BLUES
FROM THE BAYOU

BLUES
FROM THE BAYOU
The Rhythms of Baton Rouge

JULIAN C. PIPER

PELICAN PUBLISHING COMPANY
GRETNA 2017

To the memory of my friend Rockin' Tabby Thomas,
king of the Louisiana swamp blues

The word "Pelican" and the depiction of a pelican are
trademarks of Pelican Publishing Company, Inc., and are
registered in the U.S. Patent and Trademark Office.

Library of Congress Cataloging-in-Publication Data

Names: Piper, Julian C.
Title: Blues from the bayou : the rhythms of Baton Rouge / Julian C. Piper.
Description: Gretna, Louisiana : Pelican Publishing Company, [2017] |
    Includes bibliographical references and index.
Identifiers: LCCN 2016059093| ISBN 9781455623099 (pbk. : alk. paper) | ISBN
    9781455623105 (e-book)
Subjects: LCSH: Blues (Music)—Louisiana—Baton Rouge—History and
    criticism.| Blues musicians—Louisiana—Baton Rouge.
Classification: LCC ML3521 .P56 2017 | DDC 781.64309763/35—dc23 LC
record available at https://lccn.loc.gov/2016059093

Printed in the United States of America

Published by Pelican Publishing Company, Inc.
1000 Burmaster Street, Gretna, Louisiana 70053

Contents

Acknowledgments

In my years of playing blues, I have always found the blues fraternity to be hugely supportive. In particular, I'd like to thank all the musicians whom I interviewed and who freely gave me their time. In the U.K., Mike Vernon, John Broven, Cilla Huggins, Dave Williams of BSW, and Dave Peabody were all helpful at different times, putting me on the right track.

I could never have anticipated the friendship that the late Tabby Thomas and his family, particularly his son Chris, extended to me, making me welcome in an environment where I was often totally out of my depth.

I am also grateful to Silas Hogan, his family, and the musicians who freely gave of their time and enthusiasm in the recording of *The Godfather* in Chimes Street Studios, Baton Rouge.

Almost all the interview material in this book is derived from tapes I recorded in 1987-88. Where this is not the case, I have duly credited the sources.

Similarly, most of the photographs are from my private collection, many of these being given to me during my stay in Baton Rouge. I'm unable to identify every generous photographer, but I offer them my gratitude. I must also acknowledge Paul Harris, who unfailingly popped up at gigs during our U.K. blues tours with a camera and supplied several of the photographs herein.

My thanks are also due to Brett Bonner of *Living Blues* magazine, Rand Dotson of Louisiana State University Press, and Paula O'Connor at Flat Town Music Company.

And I shouldn't leave out my mother, Vera Read, who took me to see my first rock 'n' roll show and bought me my first record—the Shadows—and my first Selmer three-watt amplifier. All helped to push me along the path.

Then, of course, I offer my thanks to Cathy, Sam, and Lucy for their patience in putting up with what at times must have seemed an unusual obsession with blues music.

Introduction

Baton Rouge August 1987

Bad luck and trouble follow me from door to door. . . .
If bad luck ain't gonna change, won't be back no more.

The air throbs with electric twelve-bar blues, a buzz-saw guitar
wrapped around a voice singing in a growl of hopelessness. Across the
street, a raccoon slinks around the scrub, and garbage burning in an
oil drum sends a thin plume of blue smoke curling into the night sky.
The raccoon's about the only thing moving on North Boulevard
tonight; the road's deserted. There are no streetlights, only the glare

The Blues Box, 1989 (Author's Collection)

9

from Church's Chicken denting shadows heavy as lead and a red glimmer from a flickering Budweiser sign on the Blues Box. I stand trying to muster the courage to cross the road, but the couple of guys loudly cussing each other out by the club's door hardly make this an inviting option. But I'd come looking for the blues, and there's no mistaking I've found it.

I'd flown into Baton Rouge by Delta jet a week earlier, a forty-year-old English exchange student destined to spend a year at Louisiana State University. It was year three of my course in American arts at the University of Exeter, and by rights it should have been easy. But I hadn't bargained on having a pregnant wife, and reality had kicked in with a vengeance. The idea of living in America for a year on my own was suddenly downright scary.

As for most postwar kids, America had always been the stuff of adolescent fantasy, a place I never thought I'd see, let alone get the chance to live in. I'd grown up in monochrome, austere Britain during the 1950s, a land where incredibly—as we live on an island not short of sandy beaches—even glass was rationed.

The only orange juice we knew came not from Florida but in small glass bottles from a drugstore. Courtesy of the Luftwaffe, my hometown was still full of derelict bombsites, even a car journey was a cause for excitement, and the eagerly anticipated arrival of the twice-yearly package of candy from my father's G.I. pal kept us awake at night. When we occasionally waved off emigrating friends on their spotless white Pan Am jet at Heathrow, we probably experienced the same emotions as relatives of convicts shipped to Australia in the 1800s. You really couldn't imagine you'd ever see these people again.

Then came rock 'n' roll, and my teenage skies gradually lightened. My friends and I listened to new messiahs—the hellfire raving of Little Richard, Jerry Lee Lewis, Chuck Berry, and Eddie Cochran—on records played by Radio Luxembourg, a commercial station free from the British Broadcasting Corporation stranglehold on the airwaves. Liberated from Tin Pan Alley's diet of songs about moonlight, South Sea islands, stardust, and roses, the songs that had held my mother in thrall, and the neat suited men massacring trad jazz, we became converts to a new religion that preached tales of hamburgers sizzling on open grills night and day. This was dangerous music performed by singers who acted as though they'd just teleported in from outer space.

I heard Muddy Waters and Lightnin' Hopkins. Their songs, such as "Hoochie Coochie Man" and "One Kind Favor," were such visceral music that they almost sent me into catatonic shock. Soon afterwards, I read Paul Oliver's *Conversation with the Blues,*[1] a book that exposed the reality of just what it meant to be poor, black, and living below the Mason-Dixon line. This was a world far removed from "I Love Lucy" and "The Adventures of Ozzie and Harriet," the sterile, glossy images of America pumped out of our hissing black-and-white television screens.

But it was the Rolling Stones, bursting on the scene and shouting about their Chicago heroes, urinating on petrol-station forecourts, and tearing up stages throughout the land, who really shook things up. The game was over. Ricky Nelson, Bobby Vee, Brenda Lee, and all the others were consigned to the discount racks. Then somewhere—and the man should be canonized—an enterprising record executive started shipping in the outpourings of Chess Records. This truly was music from another planet, and with their bright red-and-yellow labels with *R&B* stamped across their centers, the records were hard to miss in the racks. I snapped up everything going: Chuck Berry, Bo Diddley, Muddy Waters, Howlin' Wolf—the obvious stars—along with lesser spirits such as Sugar Pie DeSanto, Tommy Tucker, and Pigmeat Markham. If it had that label, you knew before you heard the record that you were in for a treat.[2]

I soon owned an apology of a guitar, an instrument with a neck like a banana, and began trying to play a few twelve bars, but as Sonny Boy Williamson[3] once sagely remarked, "Those Englishmen wanna play the blues so bad—and they play it so bad." I was no exception.

Years of playing R&B with my own band followed, and finally, in an attempt to tap into the mother lode, I began touring England and Europe backing up visiting American bluesmen. It seemed the only way to really learn, and Carey and Lurrie Bell, Eddie Kirkland, Lefty Dizz, and Lazy Lester[4] all acted as my teachers, providing a tough apprenticeship.

Somehow I was also managing to hold down my university course, and knowing that my interest in American arts lay somewhere beyond Robert Frost and Ernest Hemingway, my tutors, muttering in their wisdom that I'd probably find the music "interesting," decided that Baton Rouge was the place for me.

Of course, they were right, but in this pre-Internet age, my knowledge of Louisiana blues was virtually nonexistent. Everything I knew about my intended home could have been written on the back of a postage stamp. But I'd heard of Baton Rouge's Blues Box and knew that it was run by a singer called Tabby Thomas, who'd had a minor hit record in the early 1960s with a song called "Hoodoo Party." As it happened, I owned one of his albums, and coincidentally harmonica player Lazy Lester, with whom I'd been touring Europe a few months before, came from Baton Rouge and insisted I look him up. Of course, the whole idea of walking into an American blues club for the first time was totally intimidating, but as things turned out, it would be one of the pivotal moments of my life.

Over the following months Tabby Thomas and I became good friends, and I was soon a Blues Box regular, playing guitar or bass behind Tabby and just about anyone else who dropped in to the club. As a bassist I wasn't much good, but it was an interesting baptism by fire and the kind of experience money couldn't buy. We would go on to work together in Europe, and whenever I came back to Louisiana, Tabby would call me up. The last and biggest thrill was sharing a stage at the New Orleans Jazz & Heritage Festival in 2009, something I thought I'd never get the chance to do.

Through Tabby, I got to know and play with local legends such as Raful Neal, Silas Hogan, and Arthur "Guitar" Kelly as well as the young bucks coming up on the scene such as Kenny Neal, Troy Turner, and Tabby's mercurially talented son, Chris Thomas King. Over the course of a year, these musicians and many more patiently sat down with me and told me their stories, which I recorded on my Akai tape recorder. What they had to say represents an aural snapshot of the indigenous Baton Rouge blues scene at that time, a point when traditional ways of playing blues often shattered any conventional music form.

When I stumbled into Baton Rouge, I was in effect witnessing the end of an era. The pragmatist will always argue that change is inevitable, and in a sense that's true. Nowhere is that more evident than in the progression of blues from its acoustic roots. (As I write, the very word *blues* has become synonymous with tedious guitar soloing and the popularity of musicians whose approach is the very antithesis of the vocal tradition.) But aural traditions are as important as the music, so in most of what follows, I've written the blues guys' tales exactly as they told them to me. After all, Shakespeare's work wouldn't be revered the way it is if it were rewritten in modern-day English.

And just for the record, interviewing blues musicians is not always easy to accomplish. I've often marveled at the patience of bluesmen, badgered as they are by well-meaning blues fanatics, often asking the same old questions. Nonetheless, a kind of ennui comes over them, and the stories—when they do emerge—are usually the same ones they've regurgitated countless times: tales of cigar-box guitars and diddley bows. And who can blame them?

In my case, I did at least hope I had established some sort of credibility. I had, after all, played—or *struggled* to play—blues for years. And no one could take away the months I'd spent on the highways of Europe, playing, hanging around, and drinking with blues musicians; getting to know them; and trying to understand what made them tick.

But things didn't always work out. After several attempts, I finally got to talk to the great Henry Gray, the ferocious pianist who made his name playing the eighty-eights behind Howlin' Wolf in Chicago. When I listened to the tape of this quiet, reclusive guy, I realized I'd scored a blank. (Incidentally, my friend guitarist Martin Simpson, who spent some time playing with him, told me that Henry's best stories typically came out in the van as they traveled home after gigs. It's always the way.)

Clarence Edwards[5] was another artist I missed. I'd quite often seen Clarence playing at the Blues Box, but he was another quiet, elusive character, and somehow the chance to talk never arose. And lastly there's the enigmatic Larry Garner, who just told me flatly that he wasn't interested. You can't win them all. At the time of this writing, Henry's still out there playing, and Larry regularly tours Europe, where his unique take on the blues brings down the house.

Like all stories, this one needs to start at the beginning. So while Lead Belly and Robert Pete Williams were long gone when I got in to town—and what a buzz it would have been to hear Lead Belly hammering out "In the Pines" on his Stella twelve string or Robert Pete picking "Levee Camp Blues"—their ghosts stalk the history of Louisiana blues, and any retrospective would be incomplete without them.

So thanks, guys, for all the fine times and joy you gave me with your playing, the long hours we spent talking, and the affirmation that blues music remains the most exciting music on our small planet.

Silas Hogan at home in Scotlandville, 1988 (Author's Collection)

Chapter One

Rats and Roaches in My Kitchen

Black nigger baby, gonna take good care of myself,
Always carry a big razor and a pistol in my vest.
Turn that nigger round and knock 'im in the haid,
'Cause white folks say, "We're gonna kill that nigger daid."
James "Butch" Cage[1]

As an introduction to Louisiana blues, it's fair to say that "Black Nigger Baby," with the raw scraping of Butch Cage's fiddle and the bull-like, rough-edged, baritone roar of Willie Thomas's voice, is probably not the easiest. The first time I heard the song, it hammered my senses, grabbed me by the scruff of the neck, and scared me half to death. As a matter of fact, it still does. This music broke all the rules.

It was two and a half minutes of delinquent country blues, delivered with a crazed Pentecostal religious fervor, music that spoke more of suffering and humiliation than any God I knew. And for this initiation, I had to thank Paul Oliver. The song was on a companion album to *Conversation with the Blues,* one of the first blues albums I came across. Oliver was one of a kind, a trailblazer exploring the Deep South in 1959 and undoubtedly taking chances. If you've never met him, you could be forgiven for imagining that he was crazy. But in reality he's a soft-spoken academic who had the guts to hang out in some of the roughest black areas in the States. He avoided getting shot and met up with established performers such as John Lee Hooker and Muddy Waters, as well as obscure singers with weird names such as Blind Arvella Gray, Whistlin' Alex Moore, Mance Lipscomb, and Black Ace. In addition to their music, he recorded the musicians talking about Saturday-night fish fries and sharing harrowing tales of floods, lynchings, and levee camps. The whole package hit me like a mental battering ram.

And Butch Cage? Well, it turns out that he was probably working in Baton Rouge innocently picking up trash at the time. But as I didn't know that, he loomed as a frightening figure, a shaman from a place I'd only vaguely heard about.

To put this into perspective, in the early sixties, most kids I knew wouldn't have heard of Slim Harpo, Lightnin' Slim, or Lonesome Sundown, the Excello Records stars. There was a small U.K. blues mafia who might have known their music, but in those pre-Internet days, the very existence of blues in Louisiana was a well-kept secret. The main reason for this, of course, was that the records just weren't around. Instead, we heard the pop songs coming out of New Orleans by singers such as Ernie K-Doe, Fats Domino, and Lee Dorsey. It wasn't until the first Rolling Stones album dropped, with Mick Jagger snarling the lyrics on the band's roughhewn take of "I'm a King Bee,"[2] that Louisiana blues first hit the U.K. airwaves.

When my trip to the States was imminent, the only words of advice that came my way were courtesy of Lazy Lester. A star at Excello Records, he'd toured with my band a few months earlier and, between gigs and drinking sessions, gladly passed on a load of tall tales about the dangers of being devoured by alligators or bitten by snakes in Louisiana. It wasn't until I stepped off the Delta jet at Baton Rouge's airport, without a gator or cottonmouth in sight, that I realized that as a tour guide, Lester had been filling me up with hogwash. Ah, well.

Later, it struck me as strange that Lester never mentioned Silas Hogan in his ramblings. At one time, they both lived in the Scotland-ville area of Baton Rouge and were probably close neighbors. And because I knew he'd played with Butch Cage and Willie Thomas, I was particularly interested in Silas. He'd started out with them back in the 1930s, around the time that Robert Johnson was recording "Cross Road Blues" in a San Antonio hotel room. It put things into perspective.

Throughout my time in Baton Rouge, it was this strange meeting of people and coming across places I'd only previously heard of or glimpsed through records and well-thumbed books that always knocked me sideways. The experience of myth becoming reality was at times hard to embrace. It's probably how American tourists feel when they come to Plymouth, England and visit the seaweed-festooned Mayflower Steps, the spot where the Pilgrims first embarked for the New World.

That's how it was for me the first night I caught Silas Hogan in action at the Blues Box. The whole thing was quite surreal. Here was this quiet-mannered, silver-haired man, a musician who'd once run around with guys singing songs dating back to slavery and whose grandparents had certainly been slaves.

His close friend Arthur "Guitar" Kelly came from the same rural background, and he and Silas were the oldest bluesmen still playing in town. They both played electric guitars but in a rudimentary fashion, and to young Louisiana State University kids who saw them, they must have seemed like musical dinosaurs. Visually they were an unlikely pair. Silas was a tall, erect, grey-haired man with the measured confidence of a tie-wearing, well-heeled attorney. On the other hand, Kelly, as everyone called him, was short with an untamed mass of bushy hair stuffed beneath a hat that seemed to rarely leave his head. The two were famous for their onstage squabbles but were the best of friends, inseparable blues blood brothers, and in conversation unfailingly sang each other's praises.

"Guitar" Kelly lived with his lady only fifteen yards or so from where the Kansas City Southern Railway crossed Convention Street, just a

Arthur "Guitar" Kelly outside the Blues Box, 1988 (Author's Collection)

five-minute walk from the Blues Box. On the door to their wood-frame house was stapled a red metal sign reading: *This house is guarded by shotgun three nights a week—you guess which three!*

Sadly, the notice served as a minimal deterrent. Shortly after we first met, one night while onstage at the Blues Box, Kelly received a message that his house was being burgled. He ran the 400 yards home as fast as a man of sixty-five was able, and for his pains he received a bullet in his thigh.

A taciturn man, Guitar Kelly was not given to long conversations. When he did speak, it was in a broad Louisiana country drawl that, for anyone unaccustomed to it, was almost impossible to decipher. He spoke in short bursts, smiling almost as if he couldn't believe what he was saying. And once he started, you sometimes felt as though you might be the first person who asked him something. But most of all, Kelly loved to play guitar. Whether he knew any other keys we'll never know, but everything seemed to be in the key of E. Hunched over his battered Les Paul copy or a scratched-up, one-pickup Fender, he poured out twelve-bar blues like molten lead, a potent mixture of Lightnin' Slim and Lightnin' Hopkins: *I got a funny feeling my baby don't want me no more. . . .* They were simple songs that had no beginning and often no end, dragging on long after the dancers in the Blues Box had given up. A frustrated Tabby Thomas would wave up from the bar shouting, "Kelly, Kelly—that's it. Stop." Kelly never seemed to take any notice.

Not much is known about Guitar Kelly, but what is certain is that he was born on November 14, 1924, in Clinton, a small country town not far from the Mississippi border. Like most country bluesmen, he began his career playing for small country dances.

One balmy fall day, Kelly and I went to LSU's small recording studio and recorded a few songs. He told me his story.

"My brother had a little Stella guitar[3]; used to leave it on the top of one of those ol' armoires. I'd get a chair and put it up there and get it. Then once I broke a string and that's how he found out I'd been foolin' with it while he was gone. 'Man, you been messing with my guitar? Well, if you want it that bad, guess you better have it.' I'd sit down and try and play it, you know, and finally I hit a little tune called 'Shake, baby, I'm gonna buy you a beaded dress; if you don't shake you're gonna wear gingham like the rest. . . .'

"Finally I got to playin' it right and my brother would take me round to these ol' country suppers. I'd sit and listen to him play, but my mother wouldn't let me go. Now my brother, he played blues but he played it fast; weren't no rock 'n' roll but it was fast. I always called it the 'lowdown blues' back then, and that's what people wanted to hear. The dances would last till daylight, and everybody would just be playing little regular guitars; wasn't any electricity. But it sounded so good. You could be way down the road somewhere and it would sound like it was electric, but it wasn't. That was just the way they made guitars back then; the sound was really loud.

"When I finally got to playing I was out in Wakefield, St. Francisville, Clinton, and a big place called Rogers Inn; they were all joints, cafes and joints all in one. I played a place up in Scotlandville called the Sticks; played there for four years. But driving home used to make me feel sick, so I tol' my old lady that I couldn't make it back. But then I found out my car had a leak in the exhaust and that's all it was; kept getting sick at the side of the road every time.

"I met Silas [Hogan] up in Baker. Used to go down to his house and I'd listen to them practicing. At that time I was already playin' but just with a drummer—small juke joints.

"But Silas had four or five people in his band, and I'd just go round with them when I wasn't playing. As it ended up, me and him were together seventeen years, got to be.

"Used to be a joint up in Scotlandville called the Hole in the Wall, and the white guy that owned it wanted me to run it for him. I said, 'I ain't ever run any joint—nuff to worry you to death running a joint!'

"But nowadays they're coming back to it [blues]. Later on it changed, but the blues is here to stay; always gonna be around when the other stuff is gone. You're younger than I am—you'll see. I play blues because it's my feeling. That's what I love and always did. The other stuff do not move me like the blues. People talk about what the blues is, but if you've got a friend or your lady got a man friend—your woman, you wanna see her and [when] you can't, you gets worried. You wanna be around her. That's what the blues is, that's all.

"When you take the old 'Ramblin' Blues,' that's what it's for. If you be misused like they misuse you, or she misuse you, well, that's all the blues; that's all it is. I ain't found out nuthin' like that before. I been

Scotlandville, 1987 (Author's Collection)

working hard, but that don't give you the blues; that's another story. That ain't no blues!

"I'm telling you, Lightnin' Slim said, 'The devil make you treat me like you do; it ain't nuthin' but the devil.' Ain't nuthin' but a woman want to see her man, a man wanna see his woman. That's what I call the blues. I always say that since I was coming up as a boy. The other things weren't blues; they don't move me like that. I could be layin' down in that bed, hear the music, and I'd have to get up. Then later I'd go to sleep!"

Guitar Kelly finally made it to disc in 1970 when Chris Strachwitz and Terry Pattinson recorded the album *Louisiana Blues* for Strachwitz's California-based Arhoolie label. At the time, Kelly had never appeared before a white audience or traveled outside Baton Rouge.

Also on the album was his loyal sidekick, Silas Hogan, along with Henry Gray, Moses "Whispering" Smith" —the whole gang.

The cover shows Kelly and Hogan standing around a small Fender amplifier and a bass drum, both grinning from ear to ear, probably unable to believe their luck.

About five miles north of the city center and adjacent to Baton Rouge Ryan Airport, sleepy, laidback Scotlandville has a timeless feel. The streets are lined with trees, and houses jostle for space in the wooded setting. A few blocks away from where Robert Pete Williams was once involved in a brawl that sent him to Angola Penitentiary, Silas Hogan lived in a small red-brick house. Twenty-five years earlier, Guitar Kelly hung out with him there, learning Jimmy Reed songs. Lazy Lester and Whispering Smith used to live here, and only a few hundred yards from Silas's house are the homes of Henry Gray and Clarence Edwards.

Almost all the Baton Rouge bluesmen migrated to the city from the country, and Scotlandville must have been a homey staging post, near enough to the city center for gigs but also slap-bang alongside Highway 61. Silas Hogan arrived there in 1939, working small juke joints and playing house parties. However, he'd been brought up in Irene, a hamlet a few miles away, these days dwarfed by chemical plants and often perfumed with the stench from pulp mills.

But as they say, you can take the man out of the country, but you can't take the country out of the man. The country still exerted a strong pull on Silas. Every day, with an energy that belied his seventy-six years, he would jump in his battered red pickup truck and drive to Irene to feed his hogs. He collected the feed—doughnuts, ice cream, milk, and bread past their expiration dates—daily from supermarkets around town. But Saturday nights were usually reserved for the Blues Box on North Boulevard. Hunched over his guitar, with his son Sam on second guitar or drums, he conjured up blues magic unchanged since the days of Jimmy Reed and Lightnin' Hopkins, a time when the sounds of Fleetwood Mac or Aerosmith would have been as unlikely as a moon landing might have seemed to Galileo.

Silas was born on September 15, 1911, in Westover, a hamlet six or seven miles west of Baton Rouge, on the edge of Cajun country. When he was two years old, his father left the sugar mill where he was working, and his family moved to Irene, where they eked out an existence sharecropping.

"My daddy used to grow cotton mostly but also sweet potatoes, greens, beans—all like that. He had twenty acres, which was about all the land he could manage to work. I had four brothers and sisters and we all used to work on the land. It had to be that way; we had no money to pay anybody!

"They were hard times to be living. We had to grow or make everything we ate. If we didn't, then we didn't have anything. Used to raise hawgs back then to kill 'em, make lard to cook with and put it in cans, salt a barrel of pork down.

"First blues I heard on record was Blind Lemon [Jefferson], but I started playing guitar because my daddy used to play. He used to play in all different tunings, crossnote tuning[4] and Spanish,[5] played with a knife too. Nobody around could play like that except Frank Metty, the man that taught my father. I don't know where he got the idea of using the knife from, though. We didn't see too many people passing through.

"There was this one guy called 'Noon,' came from across the river where my daddy used to work. I've seen him when he broke a string get a ladies' hairpin and tie it together because he didn't have no spare string. Anyway, I used to sit on our porch 'cross from Devil's Swamp, fighting back mosquitos and hittin' on that guitar. My ma used to play some church songs, but the very first things I learnt was things like 'When the Saints Go Marching In' and a song called 'Gambling Man.' I couldn't play with my fingers too good when I started, so I used a knife or bottle to fret the strings with.

What has a poor man got, gamble all night long,
Gamble till the break of day?
He roll away from the table
And throw his dice and cards away.

"Church people don't believe in gambling or nuthin' like that, but I used to go to church with my mama, and I still go to my wife's church every Sunday. But I still prefer to play them blues! I used to kind of play the tune on the guitar while I was singing; used to play in crossnote because it sounded better that way. You could play more strings together.

"When I started out, I used to play them house parties. You got a dollar and a half. You'd start early, about eight o'clock, and play all night; wouldn't come back till Sunday morning. 'Course, it wasn't electric then but I used to use what they called a jazz horn, a trumpet mouthpiece with a piece of paper stretched across it; believe nowadays they call it a kazoo. Used to play it and holler now and then, nuthin' but the guitar and Jew's harp. Some guys used to play a bit of harmonica but not like they do now. They never knew that kind of sound was ever in a harp! Nobody could blow it and get that kind of sound back then."

While living in the country, Silas first came into contact with Robert Pete Williams and the eccentric Butch Cage and Willie Thomas. He didn't regard that as particularly noteworthy; they were just other local musicians.

Lured by the prospect of well-paid employment in Baton Rouge, like tens of thousands of other subsistence farmers, Silas Hogan left Irene and moved to Scotlandville. Silas remembered the area being full of trees and rabbits at that time, almost as rural as Irene. He began working for the Exxon oil company based in Port Allen, the nation's second-largest oil refinery, and stayed with them until his retirement in 1972.

"There was clubs all over here," he remembered. "And downtown in the fifties, people was beggin' and callin' out fer bands. Used to play up in St. Francisville, Clinton, Jackson—jest about everywhere they wanted to hear them blues. We used to get together and I'd play Friday on North Arcadian [Acadian] and also Saturday evening between four and eight o'clock. Then we'd go on up to Clinton and play there from nine o'clock till one. On a Sunday maybe I'd play at Parker's Bar but not after . . . a man got shot, killed. Scared a lot of people off, but we got 'em back. They didn't come back quick though!"

Silas Hogan's early bands generally consisted of himself on guitar, Sylvester Buckley on harmonica, Jimmy Dotson on drums, and either Guitar Kelly or Isaiah Chapman on second guitar. The electric Fender bass was still a rarity, so like most Louisiana blues bands at that time,

Silas's had no bass player, the bass lines being played on the bottom strings of the rhythm guitar. His early records for the Excello label owed much to the laconic, laidback style of Jimmy Reed and Lightnin' Slim, rarely getting out of second gear.

In John Broven's book *South to Louisiana: The Music of the Cajun Bayous,* Jimmy Dotson recalled:

"I played with Silas Hogan and the Rhythm Ramblers for about six years. We never did change musicians.

"During that time we would play a song exactly like the record or we wouldn't play it. It had to sound just like the record; that was the Rhythm Ramblers' trademark. We played all the local spots around town, across the river in Port Allen, right up to the state line in Mississippi. One day we had a battle-of-the-blues contest with Big Poppa and the Canecutters out from Donaldsonville, at a place called Champ's Honeydripper Club, where they were looking for a regular band to play on Sundays.

"Big Poppa had a way of blowing two harmonicas at once. He could blow one with his mouth and one with his nose. They played so fantastic that we knew we had lost the show, but Jimmy Reed had a new tune out called 'Honest I Do,' and the radio stations had started playing it within the last two weeks. So we said, 'Let's play it.' We'd never rehearsed it or anything. Sylvester hit the harmonica . . . squeak, squeak, squeak . . . and I just hit the drumrolls. And we got the show from the first few notes!"[6]

The Rhythm Ramblers were a popular act in the Baton Rouge area, but it wasn't until Slim Harpo mentioned them to Jay Miller in Crowley—when Silas was at the ripe old age of fifty-one—that they cut their first sides for Excello Records. At that point, Silas had already recorded for Reynaud Records, but his first Excello record, "Trouble at Home Blues," a chugging piece of swamp blues he'd written sitting outside his house watching the roaches running to and fro in his kitchen, became his trademark.

Rats runnin' in my kitchen,
Roaches around my cabinet door—
These rats have got so brave. people,
They're tryin' to shut off my stove.

Arthur "Guitar" Kelly and Silas Hogan at the New Orleans Jazz & Heritage Festival, 1979 (Author's Collection)

Silas Hogan at a blues revival concert, 1979 (Author's Collection)

Seven singles followed, such as the upbeat "Lonesome La La," a song he later renamed "Hairy Leg Women," and the gloomy "Dark Clouds Rollin'." But as Silas recalled, the relationship with Excello was not a happy one.

"Man, the only thing I got out of them records was publicity! I got to go overseas, but although the songs I cut for Miller were all mine, he took them all. He wanted me to cut something for him recently, but I ain't gonna do it. I think I only got about four hundred dollars for all the things I did. He ain't gonna give you nuthin'!"

After severing his relationship with Jay Miller, Silas cropped up on various compilations of Baton Rouge blues, notably an album for the Blue Horizon label organized by English producer Mike Vernon. He and Kelly became regular performers at the New Orleans Jazz & Heritage Festival and were at the forefront of the local blues revival at the end of the 1970s. Joined at the musical hip, the two were almost part of the furniture at Tabby Thomas's Blues Box, and they worked with guitarist Bruce Lamb's fine band, the Circuit Breakers.

In April 1988, I persuaded Silas to make a trip to the small Chimes Street Studios in Baton Rouge. He was keen to record again, and with Sam Hogan holding down on drums, Oscar "Harpo" Davis on harmonica, Bruce and me on guitars, and David Carroll on bass, we recorded *The Godfather* for BSW Records. There'd been no rehearsal, but enthusiastic as ever and in fine voice, Silas laid down a collection of his old tracks, including "Dark Clouds Rollin'," "My Starter Won't Start," and "I'm a Free-Hearted Man." For one evening it felt as though we were in a musical time warp, sitting in Jay Miller's studio.

Silas passed away on January 9, 1994, at the age of eighty-two, and Kelly on September 17, 2001, at the age of seventy-six. Their passing marked the end of the era of real Baton Rouge country bluesmen.

Chapter Two

From Angola to Newport

"[Robert Pete Williams] really seemed to be almost a star-crossed or doomed person. He believed in every ghost, mojo, vampire— he absolutely believed in all of them. He wouldn't go near a graveyard at night."

Dick Waterman, manager

"You know, if you hit a man with a .45 and he don't go down—he's strong! So I shot him again in the heart."

Robert Pete Williams

On a July afternoon in 1964, Robert Pete Williams eased himself into a chair on the low wooden stage, checking the tuning on his scuffed-up Harmony Sovereign guitar. In his dark suit and tie, he felt

Robert Pete Williams (Author's Collection)

uncomfortably warm. It was almost as hot here as it was in Rosedale back in Louisiana, and he was glad that his straw hat kept the sun from his eyes. But it was a big occasion and Robert Pete had dressed for the part. In front of him at the Newport Folk Festival stretched a sea of upturned white faces. After hearing Skip James and Mississippi John Hurt, the crowd was curious to find out just how this latest blues discovery, a man who many knew had been imprisoned for murder, was going to sound.

What they heard that day must certainly have taken those polite college kids by surprise. After the gentle, homey blues of John Hurt, with its erratic time signatures and jagged guitar lines, the music of Robert Pete Williams cut like a knife.

America has long relied upon the South to produce musical genius. Maybe it's a combination of the region's extreme humidity and the potential for brutality around any corner. Whatever the reason, the talent that has spilled out from below the Mason-Dixon line is undeniable. But committing murder has never been a good idea, the unenviable outcome generally being a life term breaking rocks on the chain gang or sweating in the fields of a penitentiary farm.

So the stories of Robert Pete Williams, and his musical forebear Lead Belly, are quite remarkable. Both escaped the clutches of Angola Penitentiary, one of the most notorious in the country, long before their sentences were up.

When I started checking out blues music around Baton Rouge, strangely there was no evidence of any acoustic tradition. None of the musicians I met spoke of Lead Belly or Robert Pete Williams. It was as though blues had started when Lightnin' Slim recorded in the 1950s. So it's ironic that, in Robert Pete Williams and Lead Belly, Louisiana has given us two of the most notable stylists of the acoustic blues genre. And while neither man can claim to have been haunted by a hellhound on their trail, their stories are every bit as unusual as Robert Johnson's.

Robert Pete Williams was a musician in a field of one, hammering out "trance blues" before the term had even been invented. His repetitive, drone-like guitar licks, improvised verses, and African-sounding harmonies were so unique that they defied categorization. With most acoustic bluesmen, it's relatively easy to detect where they're coming from—the music they've listened to and the singers they've copied. Robert Johnson, despite his much-vaunted genius, was totally a product of his musical heritage.

But with Robert Pete, it was as though he'd existed in some kind of musical void, a space insulated from whatever else might have been going on around him, with none of the usual touchstones anywhere in evidence. His raw music was scary as hell and unlike any blues that had come before.

People who knew him say he lived an ordered, quiet existence. He was a family man who stated he was aiming to "give up playing music" and was "thinkin' about preparing my soul for Jesus."

Lead Belly was a different kettle of fish: a bayou brawler with awesome physical strength, an omnipresent folding knife, a hair-trigger temper, and an absolute inability to stay out of trouble. And musically there was none of the mystery that surrounded Robert Pete.

Lead Belly had an extensive blues repertoire, with many songs dating back to pre-slavery times, and certainly had a knack for writing catchy tunes. Numbers such as "Goodnight Irene," "Rock Island Line," and "Cottonfields" have become classics, songs so widely recorded and popular that it's difficult to believe that they were written by a twice-convicted murderer.

Fond of broads, booze, and bar brawls in just about any combination, Lead Belly was obviously not a person you'd have wanted to meet in a dark alley. Born Huddie William Ledbetter on January 20, 1889, near Caddo Lake, close to where the Louisiana, Texas, and Arkansas state lines intersect, he was a big burly boy who could pick more cotton than anyone on his parents' farm. Taught to play the accordion by his father, he soon mastered piano and harmonica, along with the big-bodied Stella twelve-string guitar, an instrument that was a perfect accompaniment to his deep, cavernous voice.

When he left home he frolicked in the juke joints and whorehouses of Shreveport's notorious Fannin Street, before moving on to Deep Ellum in Dallas with Blind Lemon Jefferson. The two men teamed up, playing on the streets and at rowdy house parties. From Blind Lemon he learned the complicated single-string runs that were a feature of his early records. The heavy strumming he employed later was probably influenced by the barrelhouse pianists and Mexican musicians he'd encountered.

Trouble seems to have followed Huddie around. In 1918, after an argument about a woman, he murdered a relative, Will Stafford, and was sent down for a thirty-year spell in Harrison County Prison in Texas. But whatever his shortcomings, Lead Belly must have had more than his fair share of charm. He struck up a useful friendship with the warden, Pat Neff. The official was so captivated by the prisoner's music that he organized Sunday-afternoon picnics for his friends where Lead Belly would perform. In a masterstroke of public relations, after serving seven years of his thirty-year term he composed a song in Neff's honor and promptly obtained a pardon.

But clearly his incarceration failed to make much of an impression on Lead Belly, because in 1930 he was involved in another ruckus at a party and stabbed a white man to death. This time he wound up in Angola Penitentiary.

Angola lies at the end of Highway 66, a deadend road in West Feliciana Parish about fifty-five miles north of Baton Rouge. In 1880, a former Confederate major began housing convicts in former slave quarters on this land, setting them to work in the fields and on the levee. Angola has long had a reputation as a legalized hellhole. Today housing more "lifers" than any other American prison, among its other claims to fame are torturing inmates and keeping Herman Wallace and Albert Woodfox, members of the Black Panthers, in solitary confinement for over forty years. As recently as December 2013, a federal court judge ruled that conditions on Angola's death row amounted to "'cruel and unusual punishment.'"

What passed for normality at the prison when Huddie Ledbetter arrived is unimaginable. By the time he met John Lomax, he'd been incarcerated in Angola for four years. And it was a lucky meeting. Trawling the Southern states, recording music for the Library of Congress, Lomax was a visionary and certainly a man with more determination than most. The rear of his car was stuffed with a recording machine paid for by a grant from the Rockefeller Foundation, a 315-pound disc-cutting recorder, a vacuum-tube amplifier, two seventy-five-pound Edison batteries, a generator for recharging the batteries, piles of blank aluminum and celluloid discs, a mixing board, a loudspeaker, a microphone, and boxes of replacement parts.

The advantage of carting around this formidable load was that it enabled Lomax to record "on the spot" and play back the results immediately to musicians, who were quite often startled by what they heard.

Wardens initially welcomed Lomax. But by 1932, with movies such as *I Am a Fugitive from a Chain Gang* and novels such as John L. Spivak's controversial exposé of the penal system, *Georgia Nigger*, penal reform was on the way, and wardens were often suspicious of any outsiders who wished to visit. Lomax, grimly warned of possible dangers, received scant help from prison guards.

But Lomax wasn't a man easily deterred. His persistence was rewarded when, on his first visit to Angola, he ran across Lead Belly. In truth this huge man must have been hard to miss, but he quickly offered his services as driver, general cook, and bottle washer to Lomax, if he could swing his parole. This Lomax apparently agreed to do, although his enthusiasm must have cooled when the warden casually informed him that Lead Belly was serving time for murder.

Lead Belly was let off the hook the following year, and one of the convict's recordings that Lomax had left with the state governor's secretary at Lead Belly's request, "Governor O. K. Allen," has long been proffered as the reason for his release. The reality is that, having served four years, five months, and five days of his ten-year sentence, he was eligible for release under Louisiana's "good time laws." Nonetheless, the myth that the song did the business has carried on over the years, and few would deny that it's a good story.

The Legend of Lead Belly, as it became known, was a powerful narrative that kept cropping up. It appeared in a 1936 poem by William Rose Benét in *The New Yorker*, in Tennessee Williams' 1957 play *Orpheus Descending*, and in the 1976 biopic *Leadbelly*, directed by Gordon Parks.

After his release, Lead Belly found it difficult to find work. He approached Lomax several times, offering to help, and on September 24, 1934, the two men finally met up again in Marshall, Texas. There they agreed that Lead Belly would for two months act as Lomax's driver and general assistant in the field.

They were an unlikely pair: the altruistic Southern paternalist and the brawling, unfettered ex-convict. Trundling around the Southern states, in Lomax's small car weighed down with recording equipment, they must have made an unusual sight. Quite who was exploiting whom remains a matter of debate. Lomax tried, albeit unsuccessfully, to commercialize his find, while Lead Belly was initially happy to "yassuh" Lomax to death.

Eventually they fell out, but not before Lead Belly had moved to New York, married his girlfriend, Martha, and settled down, milking his oppressed life for all it was worth to East Coast socialites.

Lead Belly would be the first African-American country-blues musician to appear in Europe. He also became a well-loved member of the New York folk mafia, which included Woody Guthrie, Sonny Terry and Brownie McGhee, and the young Pete Seeger. Lead Belly then passed away in 1949.

Now rightly revered as a storehouse of nineteenth-century folksongs, at one time he wasted his talents harvesting sugarcane. Lead Belly's influence today stalks rock music like a colossus. "Where Did You Sleep Last Night?" by Nirvana, "Out on the Western Plain" recorded by Rory Gallagher, the Led Zeppelin tour de force "Gallows Pole"—we owe it all to him.

About twenty-five years after Lead Belly walked out of the Angola gates, Harry Oster, a tutor in the English Department at LSU, also made the long haul up Highway 66. With him was Richard B. Allen, a New Orleans jazz historian and fellow member of the Louisiana Folklore Society. The society had been started by Oster and some friends in 1956 and had already issued some albums of Louisiana folksongs on its own record label.

Oster had requested permission to record some Angola inmates. The warden was helpful, letting him improvise a recording studio in one of the prison's tool rooms.

Lead Belly's release from Angola was legendary, and when Oster and Allen arrived, the penitentiary was bursting at the seams with bluesmen hoping to emulate Lead Belly's success. To his disappointment, Oster initially found that most of the musicians imitated many of the popular bluesmen of the era, such as Muddy Waters, Little Walter, and Jimmy Reed. But eventually he struck gold with Hogman Maxey, Roosevelt Charles, Otis Webster, and Robert "Guitar" Welch. All played music that predated the electric guitar, and the real prize was Robert Pete

Williams, whose songs were unlike anything else Oster had heard.

Employing idiosyncratic time signatures and guitar tunings, Robert Pete Williams' music was almost narrative and totally eschewed conventional blues forms.

> *I be so tired sometimes, I ask my old lady,*
> *I say, "Look here, gal,*
> *If you was able I would ask you to go*
> *Get somebody to go to bed with you.*
> *That's how tired I am, gal."*
> *She say, "You shouldn't work so hard."*
> *How in the world can I help that?*[1]

The soft-spoken Robert Pete Williams came from Zachary, a small town sixteen miles north of Baton Rouge. But at the time he ran into trouble, he was living in Scotlandville, then a bustling black suburb with a small juke joint on every street corner. His early influences were Peetie Wheatstraw and, perhaps more obviously, Blind Lemon Jefferson, a player whose music was also anchored by the intricate type of guitar figures that would become Robert Pete's trademark. But he was also influenced by local musicians Henry Gaines and Robert and Frank Metty, along with his neighbor Silas Hogan. Once asked by the late Al Wilson, of Canned Heat, to explain the origin of his music, his reply was suitably mysterious.

"It's the atmosphere . . . it's a sounding that's in the air, you see, and I don't know where it comes from. It could come from the airplanes, or the moaning of automobiles, but anyhow it leaves an air current in the air. That gets in the wind, makes a sounding, and that sounding works up to a blues."[2]

On a more practical note, he explained to the British magazine *Melody Maker* in 1965, "I can pick the guitar all the way down from the top to the bottom, and I can play any type of blues I want to. I walk all over the guitar with my fingers and I'm not worried about people who can read music either. A lot of people ask me how I do it, but when I start to show them, I'm so fast for them that they don't catch it."[3]

By all accounts, Robert Pete lived a respectable life, fathering eight children and marrying a few times before it all came tumbling down one fateful night in 1956, at a small, ramshackle bar in Scotlandville called Bradley's. It was, he recalled, a dangerous place. He admitted that were he ever to return, he would still carry a gun. His account to *Melody Maker* of what happened there gives a sobering insight into how life must have been for black people in the 1950s, living on the margins of society.

Robert Pete had his day jobs and his night jobs. For a long time he worked at the Curry Lumber Company, staking balks of timber for seventy-five cents an hour. Then he worked at the Standard Oil coopering shop, where he cleaned barrels with caustic soda, a process that left him scarred from the acid burns. But at night he played guitar in the local juke joints, and he became a well-known local musician.

On the fateful night, Robert Pete went to Bradley's to meet some old friends from Zachary. A man at the bar attacked him with a broad-bladed "duckbill knife," apparently mistaking him for someone else. In the ensuing melee, Robert Pete shot the man in the stomach with his .45 revolver and then, when this failed to stop his attack, fired again, hitting him in the heart.

It was a bad career move. On April 6, 1956, Robert Pete Williams began a life sentence in Angola. "Some of the other prisoners there had guitars, and I would play theirs—they had a lot of instruments and I played guitar in one of the bands. After the Captain knew I could play guitar, he and other guards used to call up their families, and ask me to play blues for them on the telephone. . . . They told me I had no business being there, and they would get me away from there."[4]

"The amazing thing," Richard Allen later recalled, "is that the other prisoners believed Robert Pete's story. Every one of them claimed to have been framed—they each had their own story—but they all believed that Robert Pete was different from the rest."

Impressed by Robert Pete's talent, Harry Oster agreed to try to secure his pardon. But building a case was not easy. When parole was finally granted, it was only with onerous stipulations. One serious blow to Oster's aspirations was that Robert Pete was denied the opportunity to leave Louisiana. James "Butch" Cage and Willie Thomas had already appeared at many national folk festivals, and Oster was keen for Robert Pete Williams to follow in their footsteps.

One of Oster's first ports of call for help was Huey Long's younger brother Earl, governor of Louisiana and the man for whom the word "mercurial" might have been invented.

Earl had always been sympathetic to the hardships of Louisiana's black population and was a fanatical supporter of LSU and its football team—the latter perhaps more important in the eyes of voters. It was widely known that Earl, prone to mood swings and an inveterate gambler, used his state troopers as runners to and from favorite racing touts.

In *The Earl of Louisiana,*[5] a seriously funny and entertaining book bursting with licentious incidents in Long's life, A. J. Liebling recounts a tale suggesting why Robert Pete had a better chance with a character like Earl Long deciding his fate than with a more hardnosed governor.

Earl apparently noticed in the *New Orleans Times-Picayune* that a local Schwegmann's supermarket was selling potatoes cheaply, forty-nine cents for a ten-pound sack. With his chauffeur at the wheel of his $11,000 air-conditioned Cadillac, the car stuffed with visiting cronies, and a bevy of state troopers on motorcycles clearing the way, Earl headed out to the store.

He arrived with all the sirens blowing, frightening the hell out of the other shoppers, and went straight for the vegetable department. Sure enough, there were the sacks of potatoes, but they were marked for sale at fifty cents instead of the advertised forty-nine. After Earl raised a rumpus, the luckless manager set to work changing all the prices, and the governor spent $100 buying potatoes. He followed this up with $300 worth of alarm clocks, giving them to his unfortunate courtiers to carry before also buying eighty-seven dozen goldfish in individual bags of water and two cases of discounted wine.

Outside, in around a hundred degrees of heat, Earl quickly discovered that he couldn't get all his purchases in the trunk of the Cadillac. A couple of senators and a judge were sent back into the store to buy rope to tie it shut. Unable to find ordinary rope, they emerged with twenty feet of ornamental gold cord, the kind used to tie back expensive curtains.

Meanwhile, Earl was apparently sitting in his air-conditioned seat, quite oblivious to the mayhem and eating watermelon with salt. The Cadillac by now was so low to the ground that it was impossible to pass a squashed armadillo underneath, let alone a rope. Undaunted, Earl told his judge to lie down under the car and get the rope around the best way he could. The judge got down on his knees and, as he did so, is reported to have said, "I wonder what the governors of the other forty-nine states are doing right at this moment."

Crazy as a coot? Well, maybe, but with Earl Long's blessing, in 1959 Robert Pete was released on parole. But he was sent to work for a farmer in Denham Springs—then the local base of the Ku Klux Klan—in conditions that he later described as being "near slavery." "If I had to go back again on parole, I'd rather do my time in the penitentiary," he commented. With food, board, but little pay—he apparently received seventy-five dollars a week—under the conditions of what was termed "servitude parole," Robert Pete was compelled to work eighty hours a week. The terms of the parole also prohibited him from playing music, and apart from occasional sessions with Butch Cage and Willie Thomas at their home in Zachary, he didn't appear publicly.

That Robert Pete felt hard done by is understandable. Recalling his time in Angola, he related, "You even got paid to work in the penitentiary. I came out with nearly five hundred dollars and a little money my folks sent me. What good does it do for man to go in there, serve time, and just come out with a twenty-dollar bill? He's likely to go out there and kill the devil if he saw him, with anything in his hands. This is a mean world and a senseless world."

It wasn't until 1964, when America was in the grips of Beatlemania, that after more hard petitioning by Harry Oster and Richard Allen, Robert Pete finally obtained a full pardon. His first appearance outside Louisiana, at the prestigious Newport Folk Festival, where he'd been booked alongside Dewey Balfa and some other Cajun musicians, could not have been easy. Bob Dylan and Joan Baez would be among the performers that weekend, and one can only imagine what Robert Pete, coming from a segregated background, must have made of being suddenly transported to play before a largely white audience who hung on his every word. Paradoxically, it was still less than a month since three young civil-rights activists, Michael Schwerner, James Chaney, and Andrew Goodman, had been murdered by the Ku Klux Klan in Mississippi.

With no concessions to stagecraft and a complete absorption in his music, Robert Pete appeared, to people who saw his performance that afternoon, to be in a world of his own. But it was the beginning of a career, one that would bring him recognition and shared stages with other rediscovered performers, such as Mississippi John Hurt and Son House.

Until the end, though—he passed away on December 31, 1980— Robert Pete remained unaffected by his belated fame. He lived happily with his wife, Hattie, and their kids, hauling scrap iron but rarely playing around Baton Rouge. He would recall, "Going to the penitentiary helped my music. . . . I've got to keep this up playing my guitar, because it's my life, and nobody can live or die for me. . . . I just believe in moving, because the more you move, the longer you live."

J. D. Miller in Crowley, 1988 (Author's Collection)

Chapter Three

The Record Man and Poor Lightnin'

Making records has always been a risky business, but occasionally you get a royal flush. When Elvis Presley walked into Sun Records in Memphis to cut a record for his mother, or when Chuck Berry went into Chess Records in Chicago with a song he'd written called "Maybelline," neither Sam Phillips nor Leonard Chess could have remotely anticipated the success these artists would enjoy. But they heard something they liked and took a chance. The business has always required a certain kind of person to invest the necessary time, money, and creative vision, and there's no denying that J. D. Miller was right up there with the best.

Certainly on the March morning in 1954 when he recorded a blues singer called Lightnin' Slim, J. D. Miller wasn't hoping to create the next Elvis. A forty-one-year-old rudimentary guitarist with no studio experience who'd spent time in the pen, Slim was an unlikely protégé. Miller had briefly heard him playing in a Baton Rouge radio station a week before. Impressed, he'd invited Slim down to record in his ramshackle studio in Crowley, a venue more familiar to local Cajun or country artists. "I hadn't really been exposed to the blues," he later admitted. "I'd only heard the few records I'd released on my label."

The Slim tracks J. D. Miller recorded in Crowley signaled a new era for his company and launched the career of a singer who would fast become a legend. To think of swamp lues is to think of Lightnin' Slim.

North Parkerson Avenue, with its red-brick buildings and covered sidewalks, seems an unlikely location for any record company, let alone one that produced some of the most visceral Southern blues ever committed to wax. These days, it's not something that Crowley puts much store by. Click on the town's website and you'll read that it is home to the International Rice Festival, is a designated Tree City

USA, and is the seat of Acadia Parish, but J. D. Miller comes a long way down the list.

But beyond Crowley, the name J. D. Miller—or Jay, as he was often called—will always be revered. Along with Phil and Leonard Chess and Sam Phillips, he was one of a select band of independent record producers whose vision made an indelible mark on popular music. This is all the more amazing when you consider that his sonic miracles were produced in a studio operated on a shoestring, using everything from a saddle to a cardboard box for percussion.

Lightnin' Slim's success with his first recording, "Bad Luck Blues," acted as a catalyst both for Miller to expand his blues-recording ambitions and for other artists to follow Slim's path. It wasn't long before his friends Slim Harpo, Lonesome Sundown, Tabby Thomas, Silas Hogan, and a host of others took the I-10 across the Atchafalaya Basin. Their records, drenched in reverb and made with musicians as at home with laying down a rumba as their Chicago cousins were with cutting shuffles, came to define this unique Louisiana sound.

The now-renamed MasterTrak Studio is a state-of-the-art facility that has seen John Fogerty and Paul Simon walk through its door— part of *Graceland* was recorded there. And with Cajun musicians such as Wayne Toups and Zachary Richard using MasterTrak, its reputation in Cajun music is much the same that Sun Records has in rockabilly: a spiritual home.

If you take a trip to Crowley, you can still see Jay's original recording machines, the old tape decks, and vintage guitars, all displayed on the second floor of the City Hall building.

Jay Miller was born Joseph Denton Miller in 1922 in Iota, Louisiana, a small town deep in the heart of Cajun country. When he was a kid, his parents bought him an eight-dollar guitar and a twenty-nine-cent Gene Autry songbook through mail order from Sears Roebuck.

He must have had the music bug real bad, because by the time he was thirteen, he'd learned enough chords to perform in public, and his parents entered him in a talent contest sponsored by the Dairyland Ice Cream Company of Lake Charles. Jay played Huey P. Long's[1] anthem, "Every Man a King," and scooped up the prize. "Not because I was that good," he later admitted, "but because the competition was so bad." The prize was a fifteen-minute radio broadcast each Saturday morning at eleven o'clock, and Miller strummed his guitar and sang cowboy tunes such as "Red River Valley" and "Strawberry Rum." He also made five dollars per show, a sizable amount of money for a teenager at the time. Inspired by this early success, when his family settled in Crowley in 1937, he began to play professionally in local groups.

Jay's first gig was at a dance with Joseph Falcon and His Silver Bell String Band, performing at the Cow Island nightclub, a place that lacked the refinement of any amplification. Though the group was billed as a "string" band, Miller recalled that it featured the Breaux Brothers, traditional Cajun musicians. "I'd never seen an accordion before at that time," he later confessed. "When Amédé [Breaux] pulled that thing out of the box, I didn't know what I'd gotten into!"

Over the next few years, Miller's indoctrination in Cajun music was cemented by a bunch of top local musicians: the Four Aces, the Rice City Ramblers, the Daylight Creepers. But when he married Georgia Sonnier, daughter of famed accordionist Lee Sonnier (of Lee Sonnier and the Acadian Stars), he hung up his guitar and began looking into making a career with recording.

"I started off in mono, just one track and one microphone, but I finally bought myself a little mixer," he recalled. "I didn't know anything about studio technique; back then Cosimo [Matassa]'s studio in New Orleans was the only other recording studio in Louisiana. My first record came out in October 1946 on my Fais Do Do label, and after that I took a little trip to Houston and bought a Magnecord tape recorder, a microphone, and tape—they'd just come out on the market.

"That was about all I had," he said with a laugh. "I already had some amplifiers which had ten-inch speakers, and they were considered pretty good at the time, so I set up in business. The advantage with the Magnecord was that it was pretty portable too. The first thing I cut was Cajun, six sides. One was Cajun and two were country—one song was called 'Big Secret' and I think it still is," he noted with a chuckle. "Moved about ten records."

It's worth reflecting that when Jay's recording career kicked off, Elvis Presley was still in short pants. Like Leonard Chess and Sam Phillips, inevitably Jay Miller is a controversial figure. During my stay in Baton Rouge, just about everyone I met had their pet Jay Miller story, and they weren't all good. And so when I drove into Crowley, more than thirty years after Jay had first recorded Lightnin' Slim on that balmy spring morning, I was a little apprehensive.

Notoriously tetchy at any hint of criticism, particularly the kind that he had received from various blues writers, he had probably kept Crowley's attorneys in business. I'd heard many stories from blues artists who reckoned that Jay had shortchanged them on their royalties. I almost expected to meet a guy who spoke with a Sicilian accent and came across like Don Corleone.

As it happened, my fears were groundless, and the first surprise was Jay's shop, Modern Music. It was an absolute treasure trove. Hanging above amplifiers and drums was a row of twenty or so secondhand Airline and Supro guitars. Alongside them were vintage Framus and Hofner guitars, the likes of which I'd never seen before. They appeared to be as pristine as the day they left their German factory.

The second half of the shop was given over to records. Well-thumbed copies of old Blues Unlimited singles lay in rows, uneasy bedfellows alongside Cajun and country albums and the latest Def Leppard record.

Jay came down to meet me, wearing a blue zip-up jacket. A stocky man with a ready smile and white hair combed back, he showed me around the store with obvious pride before leading the way up to his second-story office. Yellowing papers were piled knee high on the floor—files, he told me, relating to a sixteen-year-old claim for damages against the current owners of the Excello back catalogue. Like many of his artists, he thought he'd been shortchanged.

He came across as a nice guy, with a friendly, if slightly guarded, manner. His twinkling blue eyes hardened into an icy resolve, he later asked for the recording of our conversation, and it was clear he wasn't joking.

As a warmup to our conversation, Jay told me how, following an interview with the editor of a prominent blues magazine, he'd successfully sued the publication for defamation of character in Crowley's court. The editor, it appears, made the mistake of describing him as "infamous." Jay had demanded a full-page retraction of what he considered to be this slur on his character, and when it failed to materialize, he didn't hesitate to pursue a legal claim. It probably helped that he'd been mayor of Crowley for several years, but the retraction was duly issued, and the magazine was almost made bankrupt in the process. As warnings go, it couldn't have been more effective. I took note.

By the mid-fifties, Jay's Feature label had been going strong, hitting with country singers such as Hank Williams and Lefty Frizzell. But the advent of rock 'n' roll was cutting into sales.

However, entering the blues market was far from a surefire bet, which makes it even more remarkable that Jay Miller chose to do so.

"I'd recorded a black blues singer by the name of Richard King, which is how I began to get into the blues," he explained. "The first guy came from Crowley. There was no overdubbing, just straight cuts. After a while I started using a second tape recorder I had, a Concertone, and was able to use it for a slap-back echo. Then we devised a so-called echo chamber, and it worked surprisingly well. I had this guy who dug graves and [made] tombs for the cemetery to concrete the walls and the ceiling of this little room behind the studio. I found out later that a far more practical way to have done it was to have used plaster, but as it was we used cement and it just about killed us both! It worked great and was the best echo chamber I ever had, although we made it without really knowing what we were doing. But if you listen to some of my early records, I think you'll agree.

"When we started off recording Lightnin' Slim, I hadn't really heard too much Chicago blues," Jay admitted. "My thing at the time was all country or Cajun. I just hadn't been exposed to blues. I met Slim when I was called to Baton Rouge by Diggy Do, a DJ that lived over there at WXOK. He wanted me to listen to a band, and we stayed in the control room while they played in the studio, listening over the monitor. But I wasn't impressed.

"Then just as I was walking out, I heard someone playing some blues on guitar over the monitor, and that was Lightnin' Slim. There were seven or eight pieces in the band and the guitar had been drowned out by the other instruments. I asked him did he sing as well, and he right away sung 'Bad Luck Blues.'"

Lightnin' Slim was born Otis Hicks in 1913 in Missouri but moved with his family to St. Francisville in Louisiana when he was small. He eventually took over the farm, growing sweet potatoes, cotton, and corn. "I wasn't wanting for nothing," he told an interviewer in 1972. "Only thing I was wantin' was for the sun to go down so I could knock off."

Maybe because of his farming commitments, Slim only took up guitar in 1948 and, when Miller first heard him, was still something of a novice.

"He sang, 'If it wasn't for bad luck, I wouldn't have no luck at all,' and it just tore me up!" Miller recalled. "I thought it was great, and I knew right away we had something that would sell, so we made arrangements for him to come over and record. I didn't have any harmonica blower or a drummer, so the DJ Diggy Do, his real name was Ray Meaders, came and played drums—he'd never played them before. In order to get a harmonica blower, I'd heard about this guy in Beaumont from my friend J. P. Richardson, the Big Bopper, so I went looking for him. All I knew was that he was called Wild Bill Williams.

"It was awfully hard to get information from black people about other black people back then; guess they were suspicious. When I was about to give up, I asked a policeman if he knew anything about him. He said, 'Sure, he's in jail.' I had no idea what I was getting into but I went and got him out—had to pay his bail, about forty dollars—and brought him back to Crowley, put him up for the night in a colored hotel." Lightnin' was due to arrive in Crowley about nine o'clock the next day, but by twelve, there was still no sign of him. "Then I got a call saying the damn car had broken down somewhere near Church Point, so I went over there with a pickup truck and a chain and pulled them in.

"I didn't have a real drum kit, just one old drum that someone had left in the studio, and it sounded horrible!" Jay admitted as he recalled the basic beginnings of his recording setup. "But in my opinion Slim was the greatest gutbucket-blues singer there ever was—a great artist, down to earth—and I liked him a lot."

At the time that "Bad Luck Blues"[2] was recorded, the R&B charts were dominated by the sophisticated Atlantic Records of Big Joe Turner and Ruth Brown, and Jay Miller could have hardly been hoping that Lightnin' Slim would give them a run for their money. Indeed, when you first hear those raw early recordings, it's difficult to understand their popularity. There was nothing new, except perhaps the length of Slim's songs. But Wild Bill was the man for the job. Unlike the thin and carefully articulated harmonica solos by Lazy Lester and Slim Harpo that would later grace Slim's songs, Wild Bill's style was full throated and, yes, "wild." It added a dangerous edge to those languid, doom-laden tracks, as Slim's whiskey-drenched voice growled the lyrics. But the influence on Slim of other popular blues singers such as Lightnin' Hopkins and Jimmy Reed was inescapable.

Jay nodded in agreement to this observation. "I'm sure he was influenced by some of the Chicago singers like Muddy Waters, but his sound was completely different. You can compare the music coming out of Memphis and Chicago—and I know Leonard Chess quite well—and of course, there's some similarity, but I can tell one from another."

I suggested to Jay that Slim's "Mean Old Lonesome Train" was a dead ringer for Muddy Waters' "Still a Fool" and that Lightnin' Hopkins, a player Slim openly admired, provided the inspiration for "It's Mighty Crazy."

"There is a similarity in those songs," Jay admitted. "But there's that extra little touch in Louisiana records that the others don't have—I can hear it. We always added percussion; had to, because at first we didn't have a set of drums. We were a very poor operation. We used boxes, newspapers, my riding saddle, Coke bottles, an ocarina. I think that's the best thing that ever happened and what helped make our records sound so different!"

Slim would probably have been the first person to admit that he was a limited guitarist, playing E progressions and moving a capo up and down the frets to change key.

"In preparation for a session, Slim and I would get together, I'd tell him a story, and we'd put the song together," Jay recalled. "But when he got to singing it, he might do it four or five times, but each time would be different; the story material would be the same but he would have changed the lyrics. He was a guy who had to wait until his record came out to learn it.

"And it's also a fact that I'd get hold of his girlfriend a few days before a session, give her twenty-five dollars to buy a new dress, but only providing she wouldn't have anything to do with him for a few days before he was due to record. That would give him the blues! He'd come in, have the blues so bad you couldn't imagine it!" Jay said, laughing. "It was a kind of a dirty trick, but the girls went for it too; they were always waiting for the next session!"

Interviewed for the *Melody Maker* in England during his tour in 1972, Lightnin' Slim related his decidedly stress free approach to song writing. "I'd take me a pole, go to the bank, and just sit there fishing. If the fish didn't bite—I didn't care; I wouldn't have caught him anyhow.

I'd have my guitar and try to learn something new; that's the only way I could get off by myself. I can think more better when I don't have somebody to cut me off, and often by the time I got back, I'd have something together."

Harmonica player Lazy Lester, who became an indispensable sideman on many of Slim's recordings, was also a useful session player and general helping hand around the studio. That he ended up there was purely by chance. During a bus ride from Baton Rouge with Lightnin' Slim, Lester mentioned he played harmonica. They got off at Crowley, and Lightnin' ended up using him on a session. "He wasn't so great at the start but got better later. He just wanted to cut a record," Jay recalled. "I believe the first song was 'They Call Me Lazy but I'm Just So Tired'—which just about sums him up; fitted real well.

"But he's a good artist and I liked his work a lot. We backed him with many people: Guitar Gable, Katie Webster.[3] I used to write most of his songs. I don't know where the idea for 'I'm a Lover Not a Fighter' came from; I just thought it was a good phrase. 'Sugar Coated Love' was another one. The Fabulous Thunderbirds recorded it and the Rolling Stones have recorded a few. And he was one hell of a box beater!" Jay added with a chuckle.

With his records needing wider exposure, Jay readily welcomed the approach of Ernie Young, the owner of Ernie's Record Mart and Excello Records in Nashville. Young began his career with a record store in downtown Nashville in 1944. He later moved to larger premises at 177-179 Third Avenue North, which he named Ernie's Record Mart. In an enterprising move, he soon began advertising his records on Nashville radio station WLAC, where his main man was popular John Richbourg, a white DJ who renamed himself "John R." in an attempt to appeal to the station's burgeoning black audience.

Encouraged by the success of his store, in 1951 Young launched his Nashboro record label. Initially he concentrated on gospel releases, but recognizing the growing demand for blues, in 1953 he founded the Excello label. With John R. pushing his records and his six-pack specials—a kind of grab bag that gave Excello the opportunity to move out some of its slower-selling releases—sales rapidly increased. One of Young's first successes was Arthur Gunter's "Baby, Let's Play House," a raw slice of rocking, down-home R&B that reached number twelve on the charts and would later be recorded by Elvis Presley at Sun. Crucially it proved to Young that there was a market for such records, and he probably recognized the same rustic qualities displayed by Arthur Gunter, in the early recordings of Lightnin' Slim.

For Jay Miller, the association would prove beneficial. "We distributed the records ourselves at first," he told John Broven, "but Ernie's had a 50,000-watt radio station, WLAC, that would play blues two or three hours a night. Ernie Young called me up and asked how much I was managing to distribute the records.

"I said, 'Not too much,' and he said, 'Why don't you and I get together? I've started a little label and I'm looking for some blues; we should work out a contract.' I went up to Nashville soon after, but the deal we had was pretty tight. I was getting five and a half cents a record and I had to pay the artist two cents at that particular time. We didn't get any songwriter royalties either; at this time a record sold for about a dollar, I guess. I had to go to the expense of hiring musicians, so there was very little in it for me and not a heck of a lot for the artists. He was in better shape than me!

"We went along like that for eleven or twelve years and eventually I got an increase from five and a half cents to six and a half, but although there wasn't much money in it, I always thought Ernie was giving me a fair shake. The records were pressed on his Excello label, and although I still had my own label as well, Ernie had first refusal on all the blues artists.

"So as far as my label was concerned, I was only bringing out Cajun or country because Ernie grabbed the rest. There was no musical crossover at that time; you either liked Cajun, country, or rock 'n' roll. As far as blues was concerned, blacks never had much interest in hearing any other type of music, and it was the same with whites— none of them were up to date with what was going on.

"But all during the rock 'n' roll era, which knocked out a lot of country bands, the Cajun bands continued to draw the crowds. During the fifties there was a lot of interest in the blues, but it started tapering down when the civil-rights issues started happening. There were still a lot of blues artists out there but they no longer sung the traditional-type blues, and the bottom just fell out of the music. The blacks no longer wanted anything to do with the old days, regardless of what it was, good, bad, or otherwise. I always thought, 'What's so bad about good blues music?'"

The most commercial of Jay's artists was undoubtedly Slim Harpo. Two of his songs, the country-sounding "Raining in My Heart" and the funky "Baby Scratch My Back," hit the national *Billboard* charts—the latter reaching number sixteen and topping the R&B charts, which was no mean accomplishment. But possibly disheartened by a lack of royalty checks, in 1966 Harpo defected to the Excello company in Nashville.

Understandably angered, Miller split from working with Excello, and years later, it clearly still rankled. "I had to pay Slim royalties because I had a contract with him, but they managed to sign Slim because of a technicality in the contract he'd just signed with me. They put some great musicians behind him in Nashville, but it just didn't work; the music just didn't blend. I'm sure that had Slim stayed with me, he would have gone on to enjoy a lot more success, because we'd just got to the point where we felt we could market him properly. 'Raining in My Heart' did really well, and we had gotten to the point where his name meant something.

"'Baby Scratch My Back' was the second biggest-selling record in *Billboard* R&B charts at the time, something which surprised me, because I never got any money for it!" Jay smiled. "I'm involved in litigation now about that, that song and all the others! After that record we set Slim up with some booking agents—something else I never got anything out of—but I really don't know how well he did out on the road.

"He did get on 'American Bandstand,' which certainly didn't hurt him, but I never interfered in his personal affairs. Most of the blues singers had little jobs, which gave them extra security, and I guess that's why they didn't move away more or tour. If they'd spent more time on the road, I'm sure they would have done better; you gotta go out there and sell yourself to the public. If they like your record, you gotta go out there and meet the people.

"But you have to understand that practically all the people that recorded for me had never been in a recording studio before—they knew nothin'! At that particular time I was having difficulty in getting them in the studio and getting them to do what I wanted.

"And I certainly wasn't interested in taking over their management; that was something I knew I couldn't handle. So although I booked a few gigs, much of the time they were left out on the road on their own. At that time it was a lot different from the way it is now; there just weren't the same number of acts out there on the road," Jay reflected. "It would have been much easier for any of them to have made it if they'd been prepared to travel, but they just wouldn't do it. And of course, you needed a hit record; otherwise the pay wasn't that good."

Like most of the Crowley artists, Lightnin' Slim worked within a two- or three-state area—Texas, Louisiana, and Mississippi—and Jay said he was happy doing that. "When we eventually parted company it was because Slim had a car wreck in a van of mine he was using. He'd spent ten years in the pen already, and someone gave him the idea that I would send him back [because of the wreck], so that's when he left and moved up to Michigan. Of course, he was being stupid. I had insurance anyway, but he'd told me once that he'd rather die than go back in the pen. He should have understood that I was more concerned that no one had got seriously hurt. I spoke to him a number of times and tried to get him to come back to Louisiana, but although he went to Baton Rouge once, he just wouldn't do it."

For whatever reason, Lightnin' Slim firmly turned his back on the music business, and his trademark exhortation of "blow your harmonica, son" was heard no more. Possibly he'd just had enough.

But in 1970, following an appeal in the specialist blues magazine *Blues Unlimited,* Slim was tracked down in Pontiac, Michigan by blues enthusiast Fred Reif. He found Slim working in a foundry but physically in a bad shape; the high temperatures had damaged his hands, and his face was gaunt and burned almost white in places. Reif persuaded Slim, no doubt pleased to be "rediscovered," to begin performing again.

His first appearance was at the 1971 University of Chicago Folk Festival, where he was joined by his old friend Lazy Lester. And so at the unlikely age of fifty-eight, Lightnin' Slim embarked on the most successful period of his career. Reif hooked him up with Excello Records in Nashville, and tours of Europe followed, including a 1973

Lightnin' Slim in Belgium, 1973 (Courtesy of Claude Meyer/Andre Hobus)

appearance at the prestigious Montreux Jazz Festival, with Baton Rouge harmonica player Moses "Whispering" Smith.

On March 3, 1972, Lightnin' Slim played the Concorde Club in Southampton, England, with the Midlands-based blues band Tea and Symphony. In an interview with local blues musician Bob Pearce, he said, "I quit music in 1964 and didn't start again until '71. I left and went to Michigan, where Slim Harpo had given me the address of his sister. I stayed there for a while, before buying a house of my own at 179 Russell Street, Pontiac.

"I didn't much want to come over to England, because I figured they ain't gonna like it. But since I did make it, I'm glad I did, and I'm having so much fun. I'm sorry my tour is ending so quick, but I'm going to have to do a record in this country before I go back. Since I been here I had to go over and play in Germany, Holland, Switzerland, and all over the place. I'm telling you they just absolutely run me down, just got me down. I ain't had four hours of good rest a night, and I'm thinking of leaving here next week and get some rest when I get in the States."

With his ready smile and sense of humor, in his baggy suits and beret, Lightnin' Slim became a firm favorite on the U.K. blues circuit. In March 1972, he recorded an album, *London Gumbo,* at the Marquee Club's Wardour Street studio. A mixed bag, it included versions of Chuck Berry's "Too Much Monkey Business" and Arthur Crudup's "Mean Ol' Frisco," crowd pleasers that he regularly dished out.

And whatever Slim's misgivings about the rigors of his touring schedule, Bob Pearce remembers him as a charming man who visited his thirteenth-floor apartment after the gig, happily eating bacon and eggs at four o'clock in the morning and raising a rumpus with the neighbors as he played guitar and drummed the floor with his feet!

Harmonica player Johnny Mars[4] played with Slim and Snooky Pryor on a tour arranged by the Birmingham, U.K.-based Big Bear Agency.[5] "Slim was a lovely guy, always had this wonderful smile and loved the ladies. He'd get onstage, strap on his guitar, then go down to the front and just stand there smiling at the audience. Then he'd say, 'I can see there's some mothers around here raised some beautiful daughters.' People loved him."

British blues pianist Bob Hall worked on those same tours and got to know Slim well. "Slim used to stay with me when he was based in London; the Big Bear tours were run on a shoestring and there was no money for hotels at London prices. Whispering Smith stayed with our bassist, Bob Brunning, and apparently they spent most of their time in the local pub!" Hall said with a laugh.

"But Slim was an old-school Southern gentleman and an impeccable houseguest. He got used to my family and I took him to meet my formidable grandmother on one occasion. He sat in my late grandfather's chair and was harangued by my grandmother about 'them blackies' across the road and the misbehaving of their children. Slim was empathetic, and neither of them seemed concerned by the fact that Slim was as black as my grandmother's neighbors!

"On the road Slim and Smith shared a girlfriend, a young woman who traveled to all their gigs, did their washing, and bestowed her favors more or less equally on them. She was, however, a source of friction between them on occasions, as Slim felt he had some seniority in this matter. Slim could bring the house down on a good night. In the seventies we played at a college in Essex where we were supporting a well-known but highly pretentious New Wave group whose name I have now forgotten. The room was packed to see the star attraction, but when Slim went on he was such a success that the audience wouldn't let him leave, and we played on and on, well over our allotted time, to the extreme irritation of the star attraction. They never recovered and the audience was leaving long before the end of their set.

"Then at a badly organized gig at Battersea Polytechnic, Slim went on as a solo act without any idea of when he was to finish. The students were quite happy to let him play for hours without a break, and in the end I had to pull him off, exhausted."

Jay Miller admitted he was always very sad about the fracturing of their relationship. "I liked Lightnin' a lot and I think he liked me. Sure enough, one day I got a call from his landlady in Pontiac, Michigan. I said, 'How in the world did you get my number?' She said that a long time ago Lightnin' had given her my number and said that should anything ever happen to him, she was to call me.

"Well, that made me feel good because I knew he wasn't at odds with me; he was just frightened. Probably didn't help that he knew a good friend of mine was the governor of Louisiana!

"I wondered what she was going to do about the burial situation and asked her whether he was going to be buried up there or back in Louisiana. I said that if she sent the body back here, I would take care of the burial arrangements. In the end she decided that he would be buried in Pontiac,[6] but I really hated it because I hadn't had the chance to see him for so long. He was always my favorite. There was something special about him. He was so down home; every song told a story and a good one!"

Lightnin' Slim was far more than just a local hero. His influence on the Excello sound is undeniable. Jay Miller's skill was such that he didn't just find talent that was waiting to be polished, packaged, and promoted. He discovered talent in people who might otherwise have remained undiscovered, artists who might well have spent their days in the cane fields. Ultimately his legacy is a mixed one, and for every disgruntled Lonesome Sundown, there were artists such as Tabby Thomas who praised him to the hilt.

"It used to bother me a whole lot about some of the things that people say about me," Jay reflected. "But I got to checkin' around and found out that everybody that produces records gets some of this." He shrugged. "Sometimes the criticism is justified, but most of the time it isn't. And I've learned that most artists—particularly the ones that don't have success—will blame it on everybody but themselves. But if it's not in the grooves, no one can sell it.

"I've written a lot of songs and in honesty, most of the money I've made has come from royalties as a songwriter. And I'm not talking about Excello—I'm more of a country writer and had some very successful songs. Recording novice artists makes very little money. When they had those big hits, I was getting between five and a half and six and a half cents per record, out of which I had paid the artists two or two and a half cents. There was very little left. I invested a lot of money in my studios and we're still taking in artists.

"But coming back to the criticism—naturally I'm like anyone else, but I suppose as long as this business is on earth, there will be guys like myself who, by trying to help people who have a little talent, lay themselves open for criticism. I don't know how to correct that. Even when some musicians make a lot of money, they still complain and say that they haven't received what they should have from the record company.

"Maybe that's sometimes true, but every time I record someone,

I'm investing my money and my time. The only thing invested by the artists is time and effort. You win some and you lose some—but you lose most of them!" said Jay firmly.

"Most of the deals don't sell, so when you balance off the losses against the gains, you'd be surprised at how many losses you got. Every time you have a big-selling record, everyone stands around saying, 'Man, you must be making some money.' But they don't say anything about the dogs you cut over the years, the ones that have siphoned off the money. It's a very tough business, and the only reason I'm still in it is because I love it, not because I'm making money. I guess if I had the chance over again, I'd still do it, because I love the music. Maybe I'd do it differently, because I was new to the game. No one in their right mind would accept five and a half cents for 90 percent of the records that were sold.

"And right now, I'm engaged in litigation against the very company that I helped build. We're told by people that know that 90 percent of the records sold through Nashville were produced here, but the fact that I didn't receive the royalties from Nashville led to friction with my artists. The fact is that I always paid them royalties based on exactly what I received, and I have statements on every one of them.

"Nashboro was sold by Ernie Young to a company in California who then sold it again—it's a real complicated thing. But if I'm successful in this court case, all the ones that are owed money will get it. Sure they will. But I won't know until it's over how much!"

Jay Miller passed away on March 23, 1996, but not before he'd received nine prestigious BMI Awards for his song writing and a gold and platinum disc for his contributions to Paul Simon's *Graceland* album.

And he let me keep the tape.

Chapter Four

Blues at the Box

"I didn't know nuthin' about the club business."

Tabby Thomas

When I arrived in Baton Rouge, like anyone else from out of town looking for the blues, there was only one place to head for—Tabby Thomas's Blues Box. It wasn't as legendary then as it later became, but it was getting that way.

A small brick building standing near the corner of North Boulevard and North Thirteenth Street, with boarded-up windows and a sagging canopy, the club blended in well with the surrounding urban decay. Blink and you'd miss it. But I wasn't surprised; the Blues Box looked like every blues club or juke joint I'd ever seen photographed. And as I

The Blues Box, 1988 (Author's Collection)

soon discovered, the club had a special magic, especially when there was a crescent moon hanging in the dark Louisiana night, and runoff flares reddened the charcoal sky over the Port Allen refineries. When you pushed through the swinging door into the sound of blues ricocheting around the walls, you were transported to a time when "real" rhythm and blues—not the ersatz variety peddled by Beyoncé or Chris Brown—was the only deal in town. And if it wasn't Lightnin' Hopkins or Jimmy Reed up on the bandstand, you could have fooled me. It was exactly the kind of atmosphere that places such as the House of Blues have been trying to conjure up for years, but it's something that can't be bought.

Like most people, I figured on the Blues Box being around forever. It was one of those places you just knew would last. Then twenty years after it opened, despite howls of protest from musicians and fans alike, in 1999 the news broke that the club would be demolished to make way for a road improvement.

Along with Maxwell Street in Chicago and Beale Street in Memphis, both "redeveloped" with a similar lack of sensitivity, the Blues Box was another piece of America's musical heritage to bite the dust.

After writing about the Blues Box in the 1980s, I thought it likely I'd never return. I was broke with a couple of kids, and as someone who never imagined they'd set foot in a genuine blues club, let alone play in one, I was grateful for the experience and the friendship I'd been shown. It was one of those pivotal moments, the kind of thing that, if you're lucky, comes along occasionally in life but sadly not often.

I decided to try to record just how it was, putting in as much detail as I could. The "Box" may be gone, but if some curious soul chances upon this account in the future, hopefully they'll get some idea. If I've got anything wrong then I must apologize, but this is how it seemed to me at the time.

To hear blues at its most visceral and gut-wrenchingly soulful, you've always needed to catch it in clubs like the Blues Box; places revered almost as much as the performers who sweat their hearts out on the bandstand. The Checkerboard, Smitty's Corner, Silvio's, and Tay May in Chicago and New Orleans' Dew Drop Inn probably all looked like the Blues Box: beaten-up joints in dodgy parts of town where you'd make sure the cab driver dropped you off right outside.

The popularity of various forms of music goes in cycles, and that is most true for blues. Currently it's not riding high. Of course, it'll come back, but today most people only hear it in a beer commercial, with a guy in denim overalls and a straw hat chuffing away on a harmonica or some young kid twiddling on a carefully "distressed" guitar and pulling faces as though he's injured himself on his trouser fly. After all, isn't that what the real thing looks like?

Blues is in crisis, and there just aren't many of the first division left. At the time of this writing, Buddy Guy and Otis Rush are still plugged into the mother lode, but Otis has had a stroke and can't play guitar, and we've lost B. B. King, arguably the greatest of all the electric players (until age caught up with him). B. B. made an annual visit to play the Club Ebony in his Mississippi hometown of Indianola, showing us all that he still enjoyed ripping it up.

That the Box came into existence at all is one of those wonderful quirks of fate. In 1961, Tabby Thomas had enjoyed a brief flirtation with fame when his song "Hoodoo Party," a stop-time quirky voodoo romp recorded at Jay Miller's studio in Crowley with Katie Webster on piano, became a regional hit. It didn't bring him much money, but it did bring credibility.

In the years that followed, Tabby was never far from the recording studio and started his own Blue Beat label. But despite his efforts to adapt to changing tastes, recording soul songs and even the occasional funk tune, by the time of the Baton Rouge blues renaissance, his career was at a low ebb. And he wasn't alone.

The glory days of blues in Baton Rouge were the 1950s, when the city became a magnet for aspiring bluesmen. This was largely due to the success of Lightnin' Slim, the rangy Louisiana guitarist who'd hit serious pay dirt with his records. There was nothing particularly unique about Slim, however. His music was derivative, and there was certainly nothing about his demeanor to support any suggestion of "lightning."

Sung in a nicotine-soaked croak over a clanking guitar, Slim's songs rarely got out of second gear. But with jagged harmonica breaks from Lazy Lester, or whoever happened to be hanging around the studio that day capable of blowing some harp, he managed to come up with a style that sold records. His gusts of wry humor were as cold as the grave, and he openly plagiarized ideas from everyone he heard. But Slim made the songs his own, coming up with quirky lyrics and stretching them out over long, gloomy twelve bars that went down a treat.

In the wake of his success at Excello, Jimmy Dotson, Lazy Lester, Slim Harpo, Lonesome Sundown, Tabby Thomas, and many others motored down the I-10 across the Atchafalaya Swamp and signed up.

But the blues had come quietly drifting into town long before Slim really put it on the map. Country-blues musicians such as Silas Hogan, Willie Thomas, and Clarence Edwards moved into the city during the 1940s, and black areas such as Scotlandville were alive with small jukes. Some were hole-in-the-wall joints known only to locals, and as Robert Pete Williams' experience showed in a previous chapter, most were definitely "off limits" for the unwary.

Seduced by well-paid jobs in the Exxon plants, and with the R&B of Fats Domino, Ray Charles, Jimmy Reed, and Bo Diddley regularly climbing the *Billboard* charts, over the years more and more bluesmen migrated into the city. And their optimism was rewarded. For years there were plenty of gigs and good money to be made, but no one could have anticipated the ripples in the musical pond caused by the arrival of the Beatles and Rolling Stones. With the exception of Slim Harpo, who with the chart success of "Baby Scratch My Back" and "Tip On In" unexpectedly found himself a "pop" artist, the down-home blues of Lightnin' Slim and most of the Excello artists sounded hopelessly dated. Inevitably, once-popular musicians found themselves scuffling for gigs.

Of course, the music never went away, but the blues remained in limbo until Nick Spitzer, who worked for the city's Arts and Humanities Council, in 1979 gave it a much-needed shot in the arm. Spitzer commissioned fellow enthusiast Jimmy Beyer to write a booklet titled "Baton Rouge Blues" and went on to organize concerts in the city and Clinton. Tabby Thomas, Silas Hogan, Guitar Kelly, and Henry Gray all came out of the woodwork, playing to audiences who for the most part would have never come across them or their music.

Encouraged by the support and growing interest, the city held a more extensive festival the following April, which gradually evolved into the annual River City Blues Festival (now the Baton Rouge Blues Festival). The revival of the local blues scene reflected a renewed

Henry Gray, 1979 (Author's Collection)

interest in the music generally. The hard-edged retro blues of the Fabulous Thunderbirds, the house band at Antone's in Austin, Texas, had made it on to vinyl by then. John Lee Hooker had recorded a live album in Houston, and on the European concert circuit, American bluesmen and women were being feted as heroes.

Nevertheless, for Tabby Thomas, opening the Blues Box was a huge gamble. As a married man with young children, he couldn't afford to fail.

He found premises easily, the owner of a derelict store even agreeing to waive the first six months' rent. But flushed with enthusiasm and heady idealism, Tabby overlooked an important city bylaw, stipulating that liquor could not be sold within 300 yards of a school. As a school stood only a few yards around the corner, and the ability to sell Jack Daniel's was destined to be essential to the club's prospects, this was something of a problem.

But again, luck was on Tabby's side. A local blues-loving attorney agreed to represent him at a special hearing of the state liquor commission. After being convinced of his sobriety, the commission agreed that Tabby could have his license, on the condition that he added the words *Heritage Hall* to his premises.

It was a small price to pay, and once open, the club soon became

The Blues Box wall (Author's Collection)

a popular hangout for blues lovers and musicians alike. But as Tabby Thomas certainly didn't have the money to take out newspaper ads, from the beginning the club's business relied on word of mouth. Undoubtedly it was a struggle. But in the eighties, Silas Hogan, Guitar Kelly, and other musicians from Baton Rouge traveled to Europe and other parts of the States. The club cropped up in conversations, the details dutifully noted down by the local blues hounds and later printed in specialist magazines.

These were the glory days of the Blues Box. The club featured the finest local bluesmen and, while unable to pay the kind of money they might have liked, served as an important showcase for their talents as well as a second home. Gradually the club began to attract curious foreign blues tourists and, as Tabby would proudly relate, even some A-list celebrities, such as Paul Newman, Bruce Springsteen, and Mike Tyson.

But when I arrived in 1987, the club's longevity probably said more about Tabby's perseverance and hard work than any feverish local interest. I first learned about the Blues Box when I bought a copy of Tabby's *Blues Train* album. I knew nothing about him or his music, but the liner notes explained how he'd opened the club and had returned to performing after a hiatus.

When I first put the album on my turntable, it was far from what I expected. I imagined I would hear some very basic electric country blues. But with his deep baritone vocals and swinging band, the album showed Tabby to be a powerful singer in the Big Joe Turner mold and someone able to handle everything from a lowdown blues to a slice of uptown funk.

Blues Train was released in Europe on Ace Records, and on the back of the sleeve were two grainy photographs. The first showed Tabby Thomas smiling, leaning on a hand-painted sign listing the club's events, which included a Monday-night happy hour and a ladies' night on Tuesday. The second was the sign on the wall facing towards town, proclaiming in large letters: *TABBY'S BLUES BOX, Heritage Hall, Live Blues Music,* and underneath it in smaller script, *Quick Foods, Mixed Drinks, Tabby's Home of the Baton Rouge Blues Men.*

I looked forward to seeing the club for myself, but by the time of my arrival in August 1987, the ravages of the Louisiana weather had left the Box in need of some tender loving care. To one side was a patch of wasteland, a mess of straggling weeds and jagged brick foundations, and on the other, a dark, forbidding-looking café with boarded-up windows. Only the occasional swing of the door, as a customer entered or left, suggested the club was ever open for business.

Tabby would later tell me how, back when he was a kid, North Boulevard had been a bustling commercial part of town, something completely at odds with the derelict shops and boarded-up windows of 1987. On the leafy streets that ran parallel to North Boulevard, life did seem to go on pretty much as normal, with people talking on porches or playing with their kids. But with the exception of a few car-repair shops and the barber on the ground floor of the Temple Roof Garden opposite the club, the commercial area was dead, a ghost town. Even in the daytime, it was a place that could make a forty-year-old from England feel nervous.

Baton Rouge guitarist Larry Garner told an interviewer, "When I first found Tabby's Blues Box, it was in the early, early eighties and it was the only place in town where musicians could go and jam to an audience. I was on my way home from work one evening and there was an accident on the highway, so I took a shortcut through an area

North Boulevard, 1988 (Author's Collection)

of town where I didn't usually go. I passed this little place that had a sign out front that said, 'Blues Jam 2 Nite,' so I stopped and went inside. Tabby was there practicing onstage alone and the bartender was sweeping the floor. I asked what time did the jam start, Tabby told me, and the rest is history. There were other places before Tabby's, but the Blues Box stood alone at this time. The blues were making a comeback and the older black folk (most dead now) were mixed in with the younger white college students. It was great.

"The place was small, and if there were sixty people in there it was packed. It was definitely a city juke joint on Wednesday, Thursday, Friday, and Saturday nights. If it had not been for the Blues Box, I would never have met Rudy Richard, James Johnson , Silas Hogan, Guitar Kelly, Clarence Edwards,[1] Henry Gray, and all of the other players that came in there. Chris [Thomas King] was still in high school at that time."[2]

At night, you couldn't miss the Blues Box. If you didn't hear it from five blocks away, then you'd certainly see it. Apart from Church's Chicken and the liquor store 100 yards away on the far side of the Kansas and Pacific rail crossing, Tabby's flashing sign was about the only light around. The illuminated red arrow, on one of those yellow plastic signs teetering on spindly metal legs used to advertise everything from undertakers to poodle parlors, was hard to overlook. Like Larry Garner's, my first visit to the club was an experience I'm unlikely to forget. Outside in the sweltering night air, a cluster of guys stood muttering and drinking cans of beer, the tips of their cigarettes glowing red like fireflies.

If I felt intimidated, I needn't have worried. No one gave me a second glance as I pushed open the club's swinging door. Inside, a small matronly lady perched behind a card table. She wore a colorful floral-print dress, and her shining, dark-brown hair was so delicately arranged in ringlets that it might have been a wig. She smiled up at me through thick horn-rimmed glasses.

"That'll be three dollars." She waved a veined hand, indicating I should drop the money into a shoebox that sat on the table's worn green baize. Inside, candles glowed on tables, and a string of Christmas lights was draped over liquor bottles at the back of the bar. There was the shining halo of a Wurlitzer jukebox, and a yellow spotlight silhouetted three hunched figures on a cramped stage, set back and above the bar. And the music ricocheted around the club like ball bearings being shaken in a colander. A harsh, loping guitar line formed the backdrop for a deep, gloomy voice.

Black clouds rolling, maybe seems like rain . . .
Before the rain starts fallin', know I'll feel the pain.

As my eyes became adjusted to the gloom, I could see that the walls were plastered with peeling posters and yellowing newspaper

Inside the Blues Box on a quiet night (Author's Collection)

clippings. Behind the bar, the bartender busied himself with glasses and bottles, occasionally leaning forward to speak to a man sitting on a barstool. When the music stopped, I walked over to introduce myself to the stocky man I was sure had to be Tabby Thomas. He looked up and stuck a cocktail pick into a glistening curl of grey boudin sausage, delicately arranged on a plate.

He wore a cardigan and dark trousers, and his brown trilby hat crowned a broad, friendly face sporting long bushy sideburns. He smiled, eyeing me with that look of mingled curiosity and openness that I would soon recognize as being characteristic of people living south of the Mason-Dixon line.

"Yeah, maaan, we just got a little thing going on here tonight." He waved his hands. "That's Silas Hogan and Guitar Kelly you jest heard. They'll be back on before long." His voice sounded like molasses.

"You must be Tabby?"

He smiled. I explained that I was studying at LSU and had been working and recording with Lazy Lester. He chuckled, a rolling sound that seemed to come from the very depths of his soul.

"Yeah, Lester's a friend of mine. You play guitar, man?" he asked.

I nodded.

"You wanna get up and do something?" By his tone, I sensed I had little choice. But before I could answer, he turned towards Silas Hogan and Guitar Kelly, who sat quietly sipping orange juice at a nearby table.

"Where Charles at? He still here?"

Silas Hogan waved vaguely towards the back of the club. Though his grey hair poked out from below the rim of a silver hardhat, he was a distinguished-looking man, more like an elderly attorney than a legendary Excello bluesman.

"Hey, Charles," Tabby bellowed with unexpected authority. "Get back up here, can you? We got a boy from London, England wants to play. . . ."

This wasn't exactly what I had in mind. But it was too late to stop now. Charles Cross sauntered up, a middle-aged man also wearing a trilby, with a neatly trimmed moustache in the center of his wide, friendly face. We shook hands.

"Hey, man, pleased to meet you." He smiled. "We'll get Kevin up on bass."

Charles Cross (left), Oscar "Harpo" Davis (center), and friend, 1987 (Author's Collection)

A young guy wearing a white bomber jacket sitting by the bar disentangled himself from the attentions of the waitress sitting next to him and, with a look of resignation, came over and shook hands.

Tabby, who had disappeared through an opening behind the bar, reappeared clutching a white Fender Stratocaster. Stuck on the guitar in peeling gold lettering were the words *Rockin Tabby Thomas.*

"Here ya go, man—play this."

Over the months that followed, whenever I looked in at the club,

Tabby was always there. Just where he got his energy to be a full-time bartender, musician, cook, impresario, and proprietor, I will never know. It would have crushed many men thirty years his junior. But if he found it tiring, certainly he never showed it; any visitor to the club was always sure of a warm welcome. In part this was due to his entrepreneurial spirit, but Tabby also had a genuine interest in people. He just loved to talk and seemed to have an endless store of outrageous stories.

Hanging out at the Blues Box was always interesting; you never knew what might happen. And the schedule of acts at the club was fascinatingly fluid. Tabby would sometimes risk getting an out-of-town guest on a Saturday night—someone like Chick Willis, Little Joe Blue, or New Orleans harp player J. Monque'd—but most of the time he relied upon the local guys.

Saturday night was usually reserved for either Silas Hogan or Guitar Kelly, with Clarence Edwards supporting. Tabby would play on Thursday or Friday. He used the out-of-town "names" to attract a few more customers but needed his own band to fill in at other times.

For months, the drum stool was occupied by Charles Cross, a fine drummer who had played with everyone from Freddie King to Bobby Bland, and Kevin White was holding down the bass. They sounded good together and had Tabby's sparse swamp-blues style nailed. But setting the pace at the Box wasn't easy. Often Charles and Kevin would be onstage practically all night with only a couple of ten-minute breaks and would grumble about the lack of generosity from their boss. For the frontmen—who would perhaps play for only three-quarters of an hour at a time—life was considerably easier.

Eventually it must all have become too much, and after one final rumpus, Charles and Kevin both left. With an acute shortage of good drummers and bass players in the area, their departure had serious implications.

Kevin eventually returned some months later, but Charles disappeared into the night muttering about "going to California," and I never saw him again. For his part, Tabby was curiously phlegmatic and handled these defections with a cool indifference. If his feelings were hurt, he never showed it.

"Yeah, man—I don't know what gets into these guys," he would say with a laugh. "You able to get down here early on Friday night?"

Climbing onto the club's stage wasn't something anyone would want to attempt after too many beers. Assembled from sturdy hunks of pine by a singer named William Woolfolk, a onetime drummer with Lightnin' Slim and Slim Harpo but then in business as a builder living out on North Acadian Thrughway, it was probably hurricane proof. Next to the men's room, a steep flight of roughhewn stairs led through a hatch onto the stage. Going up was easy, but coming back down—especially after a few Miller Lites—was a tricky operation.

Playing, too, was not without its endearing problems. With its cracked cymbals and patched skins, the drum kit had definitely seen better days, as had the quirky bass guitar, an instrument with a neck like a banana and electronics held on with tape. Across the front of the cramped stage ran a low metal railing. In a way it was comforting—it would be hard to topple over—but being on this raised plinth behind the bar made you feel strangely detached from the peering faces of the dancers below. It was a bit like being in a zoo. I probably wasn't alone in feeling this, because after a couple of years Tabby moved the stage back onto the floor, a move that I am sure was welcomed by musicians and patrons alike.

Onstage at the Blues Box, 1987—author (right), Charles Cross (drums), unknown bassist (Author's Collection)

When there was no one onstage, the jukebox took over the show. I ran across some great jukeboxes in my travels around the South, and a good jukebox can say more about a club than any wall-to-wall carpeting. But there was never any contest; the Box had the best selection of records going.

Here's a fairly typical assortment: "My Toot Toot," Rockin' Sidney; "Three Into Two Won't Go," Z. Z. Hill; "I Pity the Fool," Bobby Bland; "Air Mail Special," Lionel Hampton; "Honey Bee," Albert King; "Stormy Monday," Bobby Bland; "You're Tippin', She's Rippin'," Ted Taylor; "Ain't That a Bitch," Johnny Guitar Watson; "Big Boss Man," Jimmy Reed; "If Walls Could Talk," Little Milton; "Part Time Lover," Johnny Taylor; "Got My Mojo Workin'," Jimmy Smith; "A Fool for You," Bobby Powell.

All these fabulous records were played and played over again; people never seemed to tire of the songs. Even more interesting was the fact that no one made any distinction among "Southern soul," R&B, or jazz. It was all part of a wonderfully colorful musical palette.

After Kevin and Charles left, Tabby had a problem finding reliable musicians to back him. Then after Christmas 1987, he teamed up with a local young white blues outfit. Initially it was a good move. The club had always prided itself on its racial mix, and many of the band's friends started hanging out at the Blues Box. But the downside was that, musically, they didn't cut it with the regular patrons, who voted with their feet.

The band did a good job backing Tabby. They had learned his material and how to adapt to his unusual arrangements. But as younger musicians, they preferred to rock it up. It soon became pretty clear that they weren't about to change their ways, and as Tabby wasn't going to buy a fuzz box and learn "Pride and Joy," this wasn't a marriage made in heaven.

After about six weeks, the LA Blues Patrol decided being a Tabby Thomas backing band wasn't for them. But just when things were looking grim, the band's bass player, Doug Broussard, left the outfit and went on hanging out at the club and playing the Wednesday-night jam sessions. For Tabby, that must have been a huge relief.

Like jam sessions the world over, those Blues Box evenings could either be a joy or degenerate into depressing ego trips. And with Stevie Ray Vaughan as the new hotshot—the guy whom every guitar player under the age of twenty wanted to copy—often the Box throbbed with the sounds of "Pride and Joy" or "Voodoo Child (Slight Return)."

Fortunately, to counterbalance these sonic invasions, there were the old-timers such as William Woolfolk to show them how it was done. He didn't turn up often, but when he did—playing drums or fronting the band, tearing the stage up in his three-piece pinstriped suit with a microphone technique worthy of Joe Tex and a voice like Howlin' Wolf—Woolfolk was star material.

So too in his own quiet way was Guitar Charles. He was also a rare visitor but a fine funky bass player, with a huge grin and easygoing nature. When he got into his stride playing an old, beat-up Fender Stratocaster, it was like hearing Lightnin' Slim reincarnated; he was note perfect. Then there were Mack, who loved to play "Baby Scratch My Back," and James Johnson, who'd played second guitar and bass with Slim Harpo and came up with the "chicken picking" riff on Mack's favorite song. A tall amiable guy, James seemed shy about playing but, once on the bandstand, blew away any guitar opposition!

Rudolph Richard, a fine guitarist equally at home playing blues or jazz, was another Slim Harpo alumnus. He'd often drop by the club, but his heart belonged to zydeco, and at times he'd put down his Gibson, pick up an accordion, and maybe sing "Jolie Blonde." Then there was Oscar "Harpo" Davis, a fine down-home harmonica player who sounded like a love child of Whispering Smith[3] and Little Walter.

Guitarist Terry Singleton played with a lot of jazz inflections, often at the Jefferson Lounge run by guitarist Cleveland Jefferson. Then there was pianist Henry Gray, who for a time had played in Chicago with Howlin' Wolf. He was something of a local legend and *the* boogie king.

All were great players, but Tabby treated the jam night with a studied neutrality. Only occasionally might he bellow at the participants to "turn it down!" He was certainly very tolerant, and it was usually left to the musicians themselves to dispatch unwanted participants.

Over the months, I got to know Tabby Thomas well and respected how he coped with the day-to-day problems of the club but still managed to find time for his own career—and even an afternoon nap. Rarely a day went by without him either working in the Box or careering around town collecting beer or ice. Keeping his head above water couldn't have been easy, as the numerous boarded-up nightclubs around town testified.

Terry Singleton and Rudolph Richard at the Jefferson Lounge, Baton Rouge, 1987 (Author's Collection)

Cleveland Jefferson in Baton Rouge, October 2016 (Courtesy of Lucy Piper)

Through it all, Tabby evangelized the cause of the blues with religious fervor. A proud, friendly man always eager to regale the visitor with tales of his own exploits, to his credit he was equally happy espousing the virtues of his peers, men whose music he clearly loved—Silas Hogan, the late Whispering Smith,[3] Lightnin' Slim, and Slim Harpo.

Another graduate of the Blues Box "finishing school" was Tab Benoit,[4] who told me how he started hanging out at Tabby's around 1985-86 when he was—as he put it—"trying to go to LSU."

"I was doing the real school thing but once I got wind of the Blues Box—that was it," he recalled. "That became school for me. I began showing up at the jam sessions and playing with all the old guys that were there. I was already playing a lot of blues-based stuff, and what I got was a lot of encouragement to go on doing it. When I was playing rock clubs I'd always try and sneak some blues in once in a while, but they'd say, 'Hey, we don't have blues around here.' But Tabby's was different. Soon as I first went in there he just said, 'Hey, man, look at that sign on the wall—Tabby's Blues Box and Heritage Hall. We don't play nothing but blues here so don't come playing any rock 'n' roll or s--- like that.' You don't hear that often!

"When I first started going to the jam sessions I'd just go there to

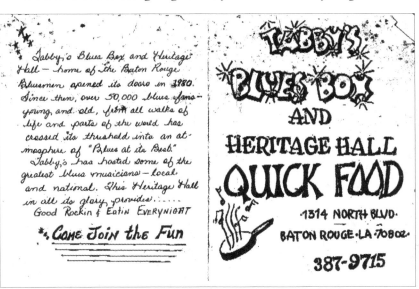

Blues Box flyer (Author's Collection)

play my three songs and hang around with all the blues players in town. I told Tabby I had a band back in Houma but when I asked if we could play the club, he said, 'Hold on, man—you gotta play in my band first so I can try you out!' I played with him for a year, played the New Orleans Jazz Festival, Baton Rouge Blues Festival, and I was just his guitar player. He made me wear a Tabby's Blues Box and Heritage Hall T-shirt—the T-shirt was fifteen dollars but we were only getting paid thirteen dollars so we owed him two bucks!

"We had to play on the gear he had onstage and if we ever complained, Tabby would say, 'Some of the best players in the world have played on this gear—there ain't nothing wrong with it.' I don't even know what the amp was. It was some kind of Fender but it didn't have any covering or writing on it. The bass had a Fender Showman cabinet with 6x12s in it. I remember the mic stand was bent, and the retaining bolt on the cymbal stand was held in position with duct tape. Sometimes the drummer would hit it and it would fall on the floor, so he'd have to pick it up in the middle of a song."

And if musicians came and went, so too did the audience. One week there'd hardly be a black face in the club, and the place would be taken over by LSU students whooping and hollering as if they owned it. Then suddenly they'd disappear, and Tabby's would again feel like an authentic black blues club. I felt uncomfortable about these student invasions, but Tabby was in no position to discourage them. At a time when the Box was fighting for economic survival, any person walking through the door was welcome, and undoubtedly the students forked out a lot of money.

In October '87, a young white LSU girl was shot and left paralyzed outside the club. It's said she and her boyfriend found two men attempting to break into her car. The boyfriend apparently tackled the larger of the two, taking him to the ground, at which point his twelve-year-old accomplice produced a small-calibre pistol and shot the girl. The effect on the club's business was disastrous; suddenly there wasn't an LSU student to be seen. But with characteristic stoicism, Tabby shrugged his shoulders and carried on. In time people would forget, and in time, of course, they did.

This continual turnover of the audience was matched by the comings and goings of the staff. A succession of waitresses flitted around the Box like beautiful swallows—one day there, the next gone.

If I mentioned this to Tabby, he'd just smile and roll his eyes. The one waitress who did stay the course was Janina, a tall big-hipped woman with a wide face and generous mouthful of teeth. She was given to sashaying around with one hand on her hip, bulging from a low-cut leopard-skin dress that clung to her like a second skin. As scary as she was beautiful, Janina would motion you to a table, throwing her glorious mane of silky black hair to one side in a manner worthy of a Hollywood casting session, and teeter over on her high heels to take your order. Ten minutes later she would be back for your next order, and you didn't like to say no. Janina was a hustler, and that's probably why she lasted as long as she did. I don't know if Tabby paid her on a commission basis, but she certainly acted that way.

It was common to hear Tabby exhorting his waitresses to "get your butt from behind the bar" and *"hustle!"* but I never heard him do it to Janina. Sometimes I thought she scared the heck out of Tabby too.

After I left in 1988, it would be ten years before I again stood on the Blues Box stage. As I hoped, not a lot had changed. There were the

Tabby Thomas at the Blues Box with guitarist John Lisi and pianist Henry Gray, 1997 (Author's Collection]

Tabby Thomas at the Blues Box, 1997 (Author's Collection)

same fading posters on the walls, the bar festooned with Tabby's albums and T-shirts, the jukebox chugging out Z. Z. Hill. But Tabby had moved the stage to the front of the club, his bulky PA speakers precariously positioned on the ledge that ran behind. I found him sitting in regal splendor, flanked by Henry Gray and a younger man who Tabby told me was acting as his valet.

Tabby had also upped his game. Since we recorded his album of the same name, Tabby was now the "king of the swamp blues." When it was time to hit the stage, he entered from behind the bar, singing through a radio mic, with another radio set up on his guitar. The young guy walked behind him, flapping a towel. The band was already cooking, with a sweating Henry Gray hunched over his electric piano, new young guitarist John Lisi[5] turning up the heat on his stripped-down Fender, and son Tammy laying down a killer backbeat on the drums.

Well, the little red rooster said to the little red hen,
"I ain't seen you since I don't know when. . . ."

All was indeed well with the world.

Chapter Five

Slim Harpo, the King Bee

"My husband used to be as skinny as a rail, so when he got his first
record out in 1957 we called him Slim. The 'Harpo' is for
mouth harp, you know, with an *o* on the end. . . ."

Mrs. James Moore

"Why do you want to hear the Rolling Stones play 'I'm a King Bee'
when you can listen to Slim Harpo?"

Mick Jagger[1]

On the small cramped stage of the Jefferson Lounge on North Street,
Oscar "Harpo" Davis and guitarist Terry Singleton are three numbers
into their set. Casting a conspiratorial glance across at Singleton,
Oscar places his lips to a Marine Band harmonica taken from a plastic
Kmart fishing case and blows the distinctive five-note introduction to
"Baby Scratch My Back." The band falls into a well-practiced groove,
and as usual he plays the number note perfect.

With Baton Rouge's long history of harmonica greats—Lazy Lester,
Whispering Smith, Raful Neal, Slim Harpo—Oscar knows he has a
tradition to maintain. As the number ends, the small but appreciative
audience at the Tuesday-night jam session roars its approval. "Baby
Scratch My Back" must be one of the most performed tunes in the
repertoire of the Baton Rouge bluesmen, but it can always be relied
upon to draw this response. More than just another blues number, it's
an anthem.

And nearly twenty-five years after it was recorded, "Baby Scratch
My Back" sounds as good as it ever did: a greasy slice of swamp pop
and the biggest-selling record recorded at J. D. Miller's studio. It was
also about the last blues track cut in Crowley, and with the ownership

of the song royalties bitterly contested, it was both the end of an era and a sad finale.

Slim Harpo had a knack for coming up with great hooks and quirky songs. Coupled with his sensuous, relaxed adenoidal singing and throaty, simple harmonica playing, it made for a winning combination. "I'm a King Bee," "Raining in My Heart," "Got Love If You Want It," "Don't Start Crying Now," "Shake Your Hips," and "Te-Ni-Nee-Ni-Nu" make up a back catalogue that would be the envy of any contemporary blues performer.

Austin's Fabulous Thunderbirds recorded several of Slim's songs during the eighties and introduced his music to a whole new generation of blues fans. But across the pond, the groundwork had been laid twenty years earlier by British bands who, knowing a good tune when they heard one, rushed to cover Slim's songs every time a new one popped up in the record racks. The Yardbirds recorded "Got Love If You Want It," the Rolling Stones had "I'm a King Bee" and "Shake Your Hips," and Van Morrison's Them made "Don't Start Crying Now" their first single release. The Kinks, Pretty Things, Downliners Sect, and countless others all worshipped at the Slim Harpo songbook.

Slim didn't do too badly in America either. Three times his records nudged into the *Billboard* pop chart. In the wake of his record success, Slim occasionally left the familiar Baton Rouge juke joints behind, venturing out to heady venues such as the Scene club in New York and the trendy Whisky a Go Go in Los Angeles. And he began to cross over into the lucrative white club and theater circuit, something none of his contemporaries had achieved.

Then in a cruel twist of fate, just when he was about to embark on his first European tour in 1970, Slim died of a heart attack. But his legacy stretches beyond his music. When the Rolling Stones signed with Atlantic Records in 1971, Ahmet Ertegun, it's said, joked that Mick Jagger would have signed with Excello Records if they could have afforded the band. Since they couldn't, he said, the Stones instead settled for his slightly less funky millions.

Slim Harpo was born James Moore on January 11, 1924, in Lobdell, a small farming community on the west bank of the Mississippi River in West Baton Rouge Parish. For the majority of black people living in Louisiana during the 1920s and '30s, rural life was tough and unrelenting. Most of them eked out an existence that was socially and economically little improved from slavery days. Segregation was total, with laws ensuring that blacks had no say in the U.S. Constitution, a situation that continued until the end of the 1950s.

Throughout the South, farming communities both black and white were divided into those renting land from landowners, working it under the "sharecropping" system, and those who labored directly for the owners in the sugarcane or rice fields.

Reminiscent of Anglo-Saxon feudalism, in theory sharecropping offered a greater chance of success. Land was rented on an understanding that the rent be repaid at the end of the year from the proceeds of the harvest. In the meantime, credit would be extended to the sharecropper and his family at the farm store. Theoretically, the outstanding debt would then be settled following the sale of the crop. But obliged to sell his cotton or rice crop at a price fixed by his landlord, often less than the current market value, and with goods at the store perhaps sold at inflated prices, in reality the sharecropper had little chance of breaking even. Most spun into a downward spiral of debt.

This was James Moore's world, as he labored in the cane fields as a young man, planting and harvesting the crop in the stifling humidity of Louisiana's summer and the biting cold of its winter. In an interview with Jim Delehant in the late sixties, he recalled: "I had a rough childhood. In the country when you got to be twelve, you're like a full-grown man and you have to go to work. Either you get a shovel or a cane knife, and you go out in the fields. I worked in the fields a long time; I'd go right from school out into the field every day until I went out on my own."[2]

And these were hard times for Louisiana's farmers. In the wake of the depression years, the state's main cash crop, cotton, fell to its lowest price in a decade. Less than ten miles from the center of Baton Rouge, like most isolated Louisiana farming communities, cars were a rarity and roads often little more than a dirt track leading to the nearest "blacktop." A place like Lobdell was really "country." The social and physical isolation of these rural communities meant that local musicians had little interaction with musicians from other areas.

As a result, most bluesmen tended to learn their craft from close relatives, local players, or, as Slim Harpo recalled, the radio. "It was my first listening experience, and all I heard was the blues. I always did like music and wanted to play an instrument, but back then nobody had any money. A harmonica only cost ten cents so I knew I wasn't going to play anything else!"[3]

Slim   estimated that he was about twelve when he got his first harmonica. Sometimes on a Saturday night, musicians walked to Baton Rouge, but usually they stayed home and had a big supper and jam session with guitar and drums at someone's house.

Leaving the cane fields behind, Slim moved to New Orleans and worked as a longshoreman. He eventually returned to Baton Rouge, where he was employed as a building contractor.

It was there while working on a church in 1949 that he met his wife, Lovelle Casey. When I met her in 1988, Lovelle had remarried and still lived in Baton Rouge. A kind friendly lady, she remembered their time together with great affection.

"I must have traveled with him for almost two years—out of state, everywhere," she recalled. "It worked real good because we were together in everything we did, communicating. But he took me with him even if I was sick. There was a time that he had to play in some part of Mississippi in the dead of winter. I had come down with a cold and I wanted to stay home real bad. He said, 'No, I'll wrap you up. . . .' He wrapped me up in a blanket and we did go—but I almost caught pneumonia afterwards . . . !"

Soon after settling down in Baton Rouge, Harpo became friendly with Lightnin' Slim. Lightnin' Slim was a likeable, affable man who by this time was already making a name for himself in the small blues clubs in town. Harpo was impressed that Lightnin' Slim was making a reasonable—if precarious—living from his music and, until the day he died, always hoped that he too might live solely on his earnings as a musician.

Lightnin' Slim recalled their time together when interviewed shortly before his death. "Harpo, me, and a drummer teamed up in Baton Rouge; we'd just play for friends at a birthday party or wedding or something like that. . . . . I taught him how to play music; in fact, I gave him his first set of instruments to play with. He could play just one number and that was 'Blue Suede Shoes.' And once we went to a dance and I let him play it slow, then let him stay off, and then he came back in half an hour—and then I let him play it fast!"[4]

By the mid-1950s, both economically and socially Louisiana was experiencing the winds of change. Severance taxes imposed by Gov. Huey Long back in the thirties, along with a world war that had demanded massive amounts of the state's oil, had brought benefits. After Texas, Louisiana was the largest oil and gas producing state in the country. The state took a levy of twenty-five cents per barrel from the oil companies, and with a daily output in 1957 of 800,000 barrels, Louisiana was collecting more than seventy million dollars in such taxes annually.

With the unprecedented economic boom continuing to draw people from rural areas into the city, for musicians like Harpo and Lightnin' Slim, these were lucrative times. The city's black residents were ready to spend their newfound wealth on enjoying themselves.

There was so much work to be had that Raful Neal remembers regularly playing eight gigs a week, three of these being on Sunday! Slim Harpo had heard the records of country singers such as Blind Lemon Jefferson when he was younger, but like Lightnin' Slim, one of his main influences was Jimmy Reed.

Reed had settled in Chicago in 1953 but was born on September 6, 1925, on a plantation near the Mississippi Delta hamlet of Dunleith. Together with his childhood friend Eddie Taylor, who would play on all his hit records, he followed seminal Delta blues musicians such as Robert Johnson and Charlie Patton to house parties. Reed later recalled that as small boys, the pair had frequently crawled under the shacks to listen to the music. After a few years sharecropping, Jimmy Reed moved up Highway 49 to Chicago and, after living there for two years, somehow managed to flunk an audition for Leonard Chess. But when he achieved his first monster hit with "You Don't Have to Go" on the Vee-Jay label, it was the first in a long succession of monster hits, which certainly must have given Leonard Chess food for thought. Reed's relaxed, simple singing style and rhythms became his hallmark. It provided a perfect antidote to the emergent rock 'n' roll of the time and, for Southern blacks familiar with Reed's musical background, struck an immediate chord.

Beyond the obvious commerciality of Reed's music, it was very easy to play. All of his numbers utilized a traditional three-line verse structure and presented no great problems instrumentally. Backed by second guitarist Eddie Taylor, Reed played basic shuffle-rhythm guitar, occasionally soloing on a harmonica held in front of him on a metal rack. He achieved a distinctive style, but as he was unable to use his hands on the instrument, the riffs produced were of necessity simple and easy to copy. Unlike the technically proficient guitar-based blues of Texas performers such as T-Bone Walker and Freddie King, here was a blues style that could be easily emulated and had a broad appeal.

Lightnin' Slim played many of Reed's songs, such as "Big Boss Man" and "Baby What You Want Me to Do," in his own band, which also featured James Moore on harmonica. Convinced of his friend's talent, Slim promised to do all he could to get Moore on one of his recording sessions. In February 1957, Lightnin' traveled to Crowley to record and took Moore with him to play the harmonica. After his session was over, Lightnin' asked Jay Miller whether it might be possible for Harpo to cut a record also. Miller was initially far from impressed with Harpo's singing ability.

"His singing was very, very poor. I liked his harmonica playing, but it was a different thing with his singing. And I've always found in music, like any other thing, sometimes you've got to have a gimmick.

"So, it was a little ridiculous to ask him to do it, but he did it. I asked him to sing—kinda sing through his nose—with a nasal sound. You know who developed that? Hank Williams."

Not for the last time, Miller's love of country music found an unusual outlet in the blues world.

Now renamed Slim Harpo, Moore cut a masterpiece. Propelled by a repetitive Muddy Waters-type guitar figure, a huge loping bass, and Harpo's voice echoed to almost futuristic proportions, "I'm a King Bee" hits you like an electric shock.

When Harpo tells the bass player to "buzz a while" and "sting it," you wonder what the heck's going to happen next.

The flip side of the record, "Got Love If You Want It," was another storming masterpiece, with Harpo's vocals and harmonica riding over an odd Latin American rhythm that's somewhere between a samba and a rumba. Just who played on the cuts remains a mystery. It is usually attributed to the Guitar Gable trio, featuring Gable on guitar, John "Fats" Perrodin on bass, and Clarence "Jockey" Etienne on drums. But Lightnin' Slim once laid claim to being the guitarist, as has Rudolph Richard.

Richard met Slim Harpo through his guitar teacher, Lonesome Sundown. "'King Bee' was the first number that we cut. I was playin' the bass guitar but I always got nervous because I didn't want to miss that run! Slim told me to do that but where he got the idea from I don't know. I'd never heard the Muddy Waters record called 'Honey Bee.' . . ."

In the den of the brick house that her husband built, a smiling Lovelle Casey recalled how the song came about. "Someone said that James wrote 'King Bee' while he was tinkering with his Cadillac, but that's not a fact. We were on our way to New York or someplace when we passed a group of beehives so we pulled up onto the side. I was amazed because I had never seen so many beehives before. So James started hummin' a tune. I said, 'What you doin'?' He said, 'I'm thinking of a song—*I'm a king bee. . . .*'

"As he thought of the words I'd write them down, and if I thought of something, then I'd do the same. When we got home we'd take what we liked and throw away what we didn't. Slim should have got the credits for that song; I should know—I wrote the words down!"

In Louisiana, Harpo's record attracted only mild interest and sold poorly, but 3,000 miles away, "I'm a King Bee" and "Got Love If You Want It" quickly became staple numbers in the repertoire of any self-respecting British R&B band.

Slim was not aware of this at the time. For him and his band—Rudolph Richard and James Johnson on guitars and a drummer with the unlikely name of Bozo the Clown—having a small local record merely meant playing Saturday-night dances a little farther afield.

With blues becoming increasingly popular, most small farming communities had their own beer joint or "juke," a place where people would gather and dance on a Saturday night, hoping they'd be fine to attend church on Sunday. Slim's band was also helped by Jay Miller's wide contacts, often enabling them to travel well beyond their home state. Joe Carl in Birmingham Alabama, contracted to have "Slim Harpo and his band, Monday November 23 [1959] $250, to play two shows; one for the white and one for the colored." Carl was to send Miller a deposit, then pay Slim the remainder after the gig, and for the time, this fee must

Rudolph Richard, 1979 (Author's Collection)

Keith Richards and Slim Harpo (Author's Collection)

have been substantial. Around that time Slim also played a concert for what was then the *very* white University of Mississippi, something of a long shot in those pre-James Meredith days.

During my time in Baton Rouge, I met many people who had known Slim either as a friend or perhaps merely as the singer in a local band. He was obviously a loveable guy, and everyone remembered him with affection. And if the "devil's music" has traditionally been at odds with religion, it didn't cause any problems in the Harpo family. At the time she was married to Slim, Lovelle Casey was a prominent member of the gospel choir in her Baptist church.

"Before I met Slim, I didn't frequent nightclubs. The only time that I did was when I followed him around . . . but before that I never did. I liked to go to church; I always sang in the choir. But between Slim and I there was never any conflict. I just said, 'I'll go with you when you need me, but you'll have to go to church with me!'

"And that's what he always did. My pastor didn't mind—he told me that it was just like he had a job. But I know that Slim *did* take religion seriously. Quite often I'd find him on his knees praying. After he got started, however much he liked playing his music, he never forgot

God. My pastor told him that just so long as he didn't put God out of his life, it would always be all right for him to play blues."

Slim followed up the success of "I'm a King Bee" with four more singles—"Wondering and Worrying," "You'll Be Sorry One Day," "Buzz Me Babe," and "Blues Hangover." All were fine examples of Jay Miller's craft and great swamp-pop songs, but none had the compelling drive or novelty value of "I'm a King Bee."

By this time, Miller's Nashville connection was firmly established, and radio station WLAC's jock Gene Nobles pushed every Excello release he could lay his hands on. Back in the late fifties, Nobles interspersed his risqué ads for White Rose Petroleum Jelly with constant exhortations to his listeners to get out and buy the fine sounds they were hearing. And he knew his audience: kids who lay awake until three or four o'clock in the morning, secretly listening to music they wouldn't get anywhere else.

But just as it was beginning to look as though Slim Harpo might be a one-hit wonder, he and Lovelle came up with an another winning song.

"James had gone to Opelousas to work at Richard's nightclub on Highway 190," Lovelle recalled with a smile. "It rained so hard that Saturday night that nobody came out, so he made no money. He called me and said, 'Baby, we didn't get no money tonight. It's raining, and it's raining in my heart too. . . .' Just like that he came up with the title of the song, so when he got back home he said, 'Baby, get your pad. . . .' Well, I always kept a legal pad with me at all times just in case we did get an idea for a song. And we sat up until I don't know what time Sunday morning writing what turned out to be 'Raining in My Heart.'"

Contrasting with the gloomy blues numbers that had proved too down home even for a Louisiana audience, "Raining in My Heart" was a complete departure in style. With Jay Miller's influence very evident, the arrangement owed more to country-and-western than the blues. Part of the credit must also go to Miller's backing band: guitarist Al Foreman, bassist Bobby McBride, pianist Merton Thibodeaux, and drummer Warren Storm. Although capable of getting down when they needed to, the players were really "country" musicians. After a simple harmonica intro that is more Nashville than Natchez, Slim softly croons the lyrics over a delicately picked guitar arpeggio.

His spoken middle eight and maudlin words have an obvious

resonance to Elvis Presley's huge hit. But any association with the Presley number—or, indeed, the Buddy Holly hit song called "Raining in My Heart"—appears to have gone completely unnoticed. (Interestingly, Hank Williams, Jr., had a top-five country hit with the number the year that Slim died.)

The song became the turning point in Slim's career. After climbing to the top of the black R&B charts, it eventually crossed over to the all-important pop charts and, in the summer of 1961, reached No. 34 in the Billboard Hot 100. This was no mean feat for a man considered by his record producer to be unable to sing and who at the time hauled scrap metal and sugarcane for a living!

And at a time when most black records were still considered outside the mainstream, even the mighty musical organ *Cash Box* wrote in glowing terms about the song. "Slow moaning earthy blues provides the artist's meat as he takes the tune for a tuneful ride. A real weeper. Tempo moves up to jet speed on the electrifying 'Don't Start Crying Now' on the flip side, and Harpo follows the combo on a rafter shaking journey. Both ends have the goods to deliver...."

The song's success was also due to the efforts of the Excello label, now aggressively marketing its growing stable of artists. Owner Ernie Young pushed the song in his chain of respected record stores, Ernie's Record Mart, and arranged advertising on WLAC, a station with considerable influence on black audiences.

And crucially, unlike the small Louisiana radio stations with their limited transmission range, WLAC could be heard in fifty states. Tabby Thomas recalled king of all the jocks, John R.

"Man, they used to burn them records on a Saturday night! Big John R. out on WLAC in Nashville used to play them blues and you could hear them even as far as San Francisco. You'd hear, 'Now we got something out of Baton Rouge—"The Hoodoo Party," by Tabby Thomas' [*laughs*]. Thing was they'd have six top-selling records at Ernie's Record Mart; they'd call it a 'blues package.' Then you could send in your money and they'd mail it right back to you. Blues was jumpin' back then."

Although the mail-order idea was nothing new—families in the rural South had been buying goods on credit through companies such as Sears Roebuck since the turn of the century—for Ernie Young and Excello, it was invaluable.

And for Slim Harpo, it promised increased sales and the opportunity for personal appearances on a wider scale than he could have ever hoped for. New York's famed Madison Square Garden and the true baptism by fire for any artist—Harlem's notorious Apollo Theater—soon cropped up on his gig sheet.

The Apollo could be particularly demanding. With audiences able to stay at the theater all day, it was customary for artists to play four or five shows. The duration of each show was short, often limited to a four- or five-number "greatest hits" medley, but competition among the performers on the bill was always intense. There was no time for changing equipment and, even had it been financially viable, no opportunity for Slim to use his usual backing musicians.

An indication of how Slim's potential audience had changed can be gauged by the fact that, at his first Apollo show, headlining was the all-girl group the Shirelles, riding high in the Billboard Hot 100 with "Dedicated to the One I Love." However an unlikely pairing this might have seemed, Slim must have cut it with the Apollo crowd, as he returned three times. But despite further prestigious appearances on the hugely popular "American Bandstand" and "The Dick Clark Show," Harpo's career slid into the doldrums. It was back to hauling scrap metal and sugarcane.

For the next two years, there weren't any Slim Harpo records. But coincidentally, when he finally returned to Crowley in 1963, in another small studio thousands of miles away, a longhaired British R&B band called the Rolling Stones was about to record "I'm a King Bee." But it would be some years before Slim benefited from their adulation.

With the Rolling Stones now singing Slim's praises, his Crowley sessions should have spurred a chart comeback, but the results were lackluster. Backed up by Miller's regular studio crew—Al Foreman on guitar, Rufus Thibodeaux on bass, and Austin Broussard on drums—the highlights were "Don't Start Crying Now," a song soon recorded by Van Morrison with Them, and a reprise of the "I'm a King Bee" theme, "My Little Queen Bee." But these were standard-format blues, and there was nothing in the material likely to match the commercial success of "Raining in My Heart."

Slim continued gigging and concentrated on his trucking business around Baton Rouge, and it wasn't until 1966 that he again hit pay dirt.

With what he called "my attempt to play rock 'n' roll," this time around he came up with "Baby Scratch My Back," a dance number featuring a distinctive "chicken picking" guitar break. Harpo's lazy, sparse harmonica and drawled half-spoken vocals and James Johnson's guitar solo completed the magic on this glorious chugging piece of swamp pop, built around a repetitive "Susie Q"-type tremolo guitar riff. Like "Louie Louie," it was one of those novelty records where the words were almost incidental. A few weeks after release, the record climbed to the top of the R&B charts before crossing over to the *Billboard* pop charts, where it reached No. 16.

That it did so—a song that amounts to little more than a languid monologue of a guy looking to get laid—makes its success all the more remarkable.

James Johnson played guitar on the recording. "He [Harpo] wrote the lyrics to 'Scratch My Back,' but it was my music. I was just foolin' around with the riff when we were rehearsing one night, and he kept talking to it. He kept on doing it until we were ready to cut it. It's crazy for anyone else to claim they wrote it. You could only write a song like that yourself. . . ."

At a time when Motown ruled the American airwaves, "Baby Scratch My Back" was voted the number-three R&B record of 1966. Once again, Slim's career was on the rise.

The success of the record also brought Harpo some unlikely gigs. On the twentieth of March 1966, he appeared at Madison Square Garden supporting James Brown. Curiously, also on the bill were Len Barry, Lou Christie, and all-girl group the Shangri-Las! Guitarist James Johnson performed with Slim playing bass but, when Rudolph Richard left, took over the lead guitar role.

"I started playing bass on guitar just on the bass strings, had a Stratocaster which was a bad box. I kept it all those years, had a jazz bass I let Noel Neal have and let Kenny Neal have the guitar.

"I think Slim made money out of 'Raining in My Heart.' He was on 'American Bandstand' and stuff like that, but the band didn't go on those gigs; he just went by himself. He was just miming and I didn't even get to see it. At that time he still played locally around Baton Rouge, and we played a lot of the universities, LSU, Birmingham, Ole Miss, and Arkansas.

"We played right through when all the civil-rights marches were going on, but we didn't ever have any problems or trouble on the road; I guess we were lucky. We recorded 'Scratch My Back' in 196[6], but Slim and Miller had problems with their contract. I think Slim wanted to get out of it but he couldn't; the money wasn't right. He didn't tell us a whole lot but always said, 'If I make a million dollars I'm going to pay you so much, and if I don't make anything at all I'm still gonna pay you.'

"That's the way he was. 'If I don't make a dime I'm gonna pay you, but if I make a million I'll still pay you $150.' But I didn't get nothing out of 'Scratch My Back,' no more than paying to play on the record. I guess it didn't bother me, but it was my idea and all the money went to Slim. I didn't ever ask him anything about it; I was just glad to be able to put the record together. Did you ever hear those little clicking skeleton heads? Lazy Lester was on that, and he played those little skeleton heads.

"We had a second guitarist—don't know the guy's name—but he was always at the studio, a white guy. I don't think it took us more than three takes to get the thing down. Slim made pretty good money from that record because it sold well, and we did a lot of shows behind it, in Miami and Louisiana. Everywhere he played there was a house band to back us up, so the whole band didn't make all the shows.

"I went to a lot of places with him, but I didn't go to California because I was sick. That time he had Sammy Kinchen on drums, Otis Johnson on bass, and I guess Jesse Kinchen on guitar. Now I want to get established, though. Some people think it was Rudolph [Richard] did all the playing with Slim; they don't know about me. I played at the Baton Rouge festival last year [1987], which is really the first time I played since Slim died. I wasn't on the Nashville recordings and I don't know who played guitar, but I played with Slim after that so I had to learn some of the parts. Slim played some guitar but he used a capo because he wasn't very good. I played with him until he died, and although we sometimes had our differences, we got along; he was a nice guy."

But back in bayou country, trouble was brewing. Involved in a royalty dispute with Jay Miller but still contracted to Excello Records, Slim surreptitiously embarked on a recording session with Imperial

Records of Hollywood. The timing might have been better. Miller was on vacation in California and, upon hearing the news of Slim's intended defection, promptly fired a legal broadside at Lew Chudd, then boss of Imperial Records.

This aborted liaison was first in a long series of disputes between Harpo and Miller and would lead to Harpo severing ties with Crowley.

"*We* never saw a statement all the time that Slim recorded with Miller," Lovelle Casey maintained. "I'm not saying that we never had any money—but we never saw a statement. I can't say that Slim got along badly with Miller, but he wanted to leave because you, me, or anyone else wanna do better for themselves. I guess that he just didn't feel that he was being treated fairly. . . ."

When I asked him about it, Miller maintained a studied indifference. "You know how the business is—when Joe Blow is not doing any good, nobody wants him. But you let him taste a little success and everybody is after him. Anyway, Slim became in demand!"

Although many viewed the breakup as inevitable, the loss of Excello's most successful artist must have been a major blow to Miller. However, both were serious businessmen. "Slim was a real friendly guy but he was all business!" Rudolph Richard remembered. "I always liked Slim because he was a straight guy—a man of his word—but he was business."

But Lady Luck again smiled on Slim Harpo. In Nashville, Ernie Young had by this time sold Excello Records and was casting around for an artist with some "hit" potential. Hearing of the dispute in Crowley, Young promptly approached Harpo. For a moment it seemed he was too late: Harpo and Miller had reconciled their differences and signed a new contract.

But despite Miller's undoubted business acumen, he'd failed to obtain Slim Harpo's signature on an important subsidiary clause. With the Excello deal likely to be more lucrative, Harpo arranged for his attorney to check out the contract's small print. He must have been pleased to hear that the agreement was completely void, leaving him free to sign with Ernie Young. Tabby Thomas was surprised when he received a telephone call from Nashville.

"Ernie Young called me, told me he couldn't get in touch with Slim via J. D. Miller but would like Slim to come up and record. He had

Rudolph Richard in Baton Rouge, 1987 (Author's Collection)

$1,200 in royalties from the Rolling Stones recording 'King Bee' but wasn't going to send it to Slim until he came up to make some more records.

"Now Slim wasn't a guy that would run to the studios, but when I told him that Ernie Young had this money for him from the Rolling Stones having cut one of his records, he couldn't believe it."

Leaving guitarists James Johnson and Rudolph Richard home in Baton Rouge, Slim Harpo made the long Greyhound bus journey to Nashville. Young teamed him with a group of Nashville session musicians, including guitarist Mabon "Teenie" Hodges, who would later back up Al Green on his classic Hi Records songs. Slim must have felt under pressure to deliver new songs, but with producer Robert Holmes substituting Nashville's technical finesse for the raw edge of Crowley, it cannot have been easy.

The resulting album, *Tip On In*, to some ears lacked the visceral magic that had made Slim's earlier records so special. The title track and "Te-Ni-Nee-Ni-Nu," both quirky dance numbers, scraped the bottom of the Billboard charts but were ultimately forgettable.

Slim Harpo in Nashville (Author's Collection)

Slim Harpo's publicity photograph (Author's Collection)

By this time, Slim Harpo was becoming something of a musical enigma. On the one hand, his songs were achieving chart success, something far beyond the reach of other blues-based black artists such as B. B. King and Bobby Bland. But as a performer and musician, he lacked the sophistication necessary to launch him to a higher level.

He began working for several New York booking agencies and, in 1968, repeatedly played at that city's prestigious Scene club,[5] often with his old Baton Rouge buddies Lightnin' Slim on guitar and Jesse Kinchen on drums. (His choice of Lightnin' Slim rather than James Johnson or Rudolph Richard must have been perplexing. Both were superior musicians with whom he was well used to working. Perhaps he hoped the New York dates would give Lightnin' Slim a springboard to success, as repayment for the helping hand Lightnin' had given him eleven years earlier.) Guarded in its praise, the New York press identified Harpo as a relic of the folk-blues tradition.

In 1968, Slim talked to *Record World* about his experiences: "I didn't have any idea how my music would take in New York. I always thought that this was a jazz town but after my first set I felt like I was at home. The audience was real sweet and they accepted me right away."

Slim Harpo in New York (Author's Collection)

Slim's existence on the fringes of the white rock scene was an uneasy one. Whatever the charms of his Louisiana swamp-blues style, it lacked the instrumental virtuosity white audiences demanded from blues guitarists such as B. B. King and Albert King. The blues clubs of Baton Rouge were a million miles removed from the urban backdrops of Chicago and Memphis that spawned the tougher sounds.

Alternately, neither Harpo nor Lightnin' Slim possessed the acoustic prowess of Mississippi Delta bluesmen such as Skip James and John Hurt.

By this point, Harpo was still in his early forties, and he was far too young to be wheeled around the white college circuit like some museum piece. And although at home his sugarcane hauling business was still going strong, those who knew him remember that a full-time career in music remained his sole goal.

Sadly, there was a hint of desperation in his next few releases, which seemed to be blatant attempts at commercialism destined to destroy his reputation with any hardnosed blues audience. The first of these was "Mohair Sam," a nondescript country-inflected number that four years previously was a minor hit for country-and-western singer Charlie Rich. Mired by overproduction, the song was an obvious attempt to recapture the feel and success of "Baby Scratch My Back" and was a resounding flop. But by 1969, and playing a sunburst Gibson ES-330 guitar with a harmonica in a rack, Slim was a familiar figure on the West Coast circuit and in San Francisco sometimes paired with rock bands such as the Illinois Speed Press.

Slim must have liked what he saw, because his next record was "The Hippy Song," an even more dubious piece of pop flimflam. The only excuse can be that possibly Slim intended the record to have some social resonance. After all, in common with black people, hippies were outside the American mainstream. Whatever the reality, artistically Slim Harpo was drowning, and nothing could disguise the shortcomings of the record.

It's no surprise that the backing musicians have remained anonymous, their stoned mayhem suggesting they were on day release from Haight-Ashbury. The record bombed, and once again Slim was back to hauling the sugarcane. At this point, he must have felt that his twelve-year-old career was on the skids. The name Slim Harpo was still guaranteed to attract good crowds around Baton Rouge, but elsewhere his star was fading fast.

Just as things were looking bleak, fate played a hand. The Rolling Stones covered one of Slim's songs on their *Exile on Main St.* album: the infectious boogie "Shake Your Hips." A deal was arranged for Mike Vernon's Blue Horizon label to represent Excello in the U.K., and it was planned for Slim to fly to London to record an LP and tour Europe. The formula had already been tried with Howlin' Wolf, B. B. King, and Muddy Waters, and all indications were that Slim would be equally successful. Vernon assembled a crack group of musicians to record with Slim: Colin Allen on drums, John Best on bass, Paul Butler, Rick Hayward, Top Topham, and Laurie Sanford on guitars, and Pete Wingfield on keyboard.

Maybe as a warmup and to get used to being in a studio again, in early January 1970 Slim took his local band into the studios in Baton Rouge. There he recorded a couple of blues standards, "Rock Me Baby" and "Boogie Chillun," together with several original songs co-written with local country singer Roy Hayes. In 1957 Hayes had achieved some success when one of his songs, "I'm Gonna Be a Wheel Someday," was a regional hit for Bobby Mitchell and later released by Fats Domino.

Slim's voice and harmonica playing sound as good as ever, but the choice of material was uninspired and lacked direction. It was the forthcoming London sessions that offered Slim a real opportunity to make his comeback. Then as he waited for his passport to be issued, on the twenty-ninth of January 1970 Slim suffered a massive heart attack. He passed away two days later in Baton Rouge General Hospital.

Like the hippies of his song, Slim was an anachronism. Lacking the sex appeal of Otis Redding or James Brown, the flamboyance of Little Richard—or, for that matter, the sheer power of Muddy Waters or B. B. King—Slim Harpo created his own niche. And not many would deny that his musical legacy is one of songs marked by a brilliance and honesty matched by few of his blues peers.

Lonesome Sundown at the New Orleans Jazz & Heritage Festival, 1979
(Author's Collection)

Chapter Six

Lonesome Sundown, the Louisiana Lover Man

"J. D. Miller, he's just like a damned serpent!
Anything he can do to bite you or harm you, he'll do."
Lonesome Sundown

Cornelius Green III, a.k.a. Lonesome Sundown, isn't the first and certainly won't be the last blues artist to allege that he's been ripped off by the recording industry. But in his case, as one of the brightest stars in J. D. Miller's Excello firmament, the story is particularly sad. Sundown's releases, such as "My Home Is a Prison" and "Gonna Stick to You Baby," were some of the toughest—and most commercial—R&B records ever to emerge from the Crowley studios. But unlike the songs of Slim Harpo and Lazy Lester, which were eagerly covered in London by up-and-coming R&B bands, somehow Sundown's recordings slipped through the net. After dropping out of music in the mid-sixties, he eventually made a comeback of sorts in 1977, when he recorded an album, *Been Gone Too Long,* with his old pal Philip Walker. But when the world failed to beat a path to his door, once again he hung up his guitar.

For many of the Excello artists, Lightnin' Slim's down-home blues acted as a creative lightning rod. But Sundown was an exception. Able to tackle most styles that came his way, he was equally at home singing straight country blues, swamp-pop ballads, and rock 'n' roll, all showcases for his warm, dark vocals and an instantly recognizable guitar style that owed much to the ferocious playing of Guitar Slim.[1] Unlike many of the Excello artists, who modeled themselves on Jimmy Reed and Lightnin' Hopkins, Sundown played wide open.

Interviews with Cornelius Green are nonexistent, and when I began trying to track Sundown down, no one seemed to know much; there was a certain air of mystery about him. He didn't show up at blues jams, and it was rumored he'd found religion or maybe even suffered a stroke. Whatever the reason for his absence from the local blues scene, he was clearly a man who liked to lie low. But it turned out that he had taught Rudolph Richard guitar, and eventually Rudolph came up with his address.

And so on a sunny March morning, I drove up to the Brandywine Condominiums where he lived, just a block off Florida Boulevard. I was apprehensive but needn't have worried.

Sundown turned out to be a tall, friendly man with a ready smile. He lived with his wife in a small apartment on the second floor. Homes usually say much about their owners, and with its floral curtains and comfortable sofas, Sundown's was no exception. The place was distinctly homey, and an old, green Harmony archtop guitar—the only guitar he then owned, he later told me—and a faded copy of an Excello Records compilation were visible clues to his past. In contrast to his reclusive image, Sundown seemed pleased that someone was actually taking some interest in him, and smiling, he began his story.

"I was born in Donaldsonville on the Dugas plantation about eighty miles from here; my mother's eighty-two years old now. My parents

Lonesome Sundown in Baton Rouge, 1988 (Author's Collection)

worked on various plantations doing what they needed to do, hoeing, cutting sugarcane, digging potatoes—whatever it took to make a living," he said with a laugh.

"We cut the sugarcane by hand with a cane knife, a big knife with a wooden handle, and worked from 'can see' to 'can't see.' My mother and father separated when I was eight years old, and when my father left home, I was the oldest of five kids, so I had to help my mother as best I could. I left school about 1938 or '39 and because I was too young to cut cane, the man on the plantation had me as the water boy. What I'd do, in the morning I'd get up at four o'clock and because I was too small to hook up the mules, I'd be down there so the men in the yard could hook up the mules for me!

"Then I'd take the people to work, and I'd use a number-eight bucket—that's a small bucket—to take water to the people that was out there cutting the cane by hand. Man, I can still see myself walking through freezing-cold ice on the ground wearing tennis shoes. When you got down there, sometimes it would be water up to your knees, but when it's real cold, the water doesn't seem cold. I'd walk all day in them wet shoes trying to make a living. They cut the cane in the wintertime, so you'd take what provisions you needed for the day. But most of the time the cane was taller than I was, so if it was cold, the cane blocked the cold air from getting to you until you reached the outside. But it was hell. No way I could go through it again.

"Women used to cut it too, and at the time, you got paid about a dollar and a half a day. You had to cut about a ton of cane, send it to the mill, and every load would be weighed. I've seen days that I don't even care to remember."

One of the first records Sundown recalls hearing was "Can I Play with Your Poodle?," a risqué hokum blues recorded by Tampa Red in 1942. The song was hugely popular and later covered by Houston's Lightnin' Hopkins.

"My mama used to go out to Saturday-night boogies; to play the jukebox was a nickel for each record. I remember my mama used to like this one record, 'Let Me Play with Your Poodle?,' a song I always wanted to record.

Your little poodle got that long black curly hair,

Cute little face jest like a teddy bear.
Can I play with your poodle?

"They was good times. Way back yonder—I must have been eight or nine years old—a fifth of wine wasn't but fifty cents; at least two people could get a good hit out of it. But that was still quite a lot of money then. I remember if someone gave me a nickel, I could go down to the store and eat candy all day! But my daddy loved the blues, and he would sing when he was plowing with the tractor. I'd sit between his knees listening, and before he left home, we were doing good. When he left we were on the welfare, and about every month a truck would come around, give us prunes, raisins, cabbage—just give it to us, to try to help us survive. The depression was really something else, but when I had arthritis some time ago and a stroke, I needed some provisions but didn't get anything!

"How I got interested in guitar was one night I was going home through the plantation houses after work, and I saw my cousin sitting on his porch with a guitar in his hand. I said to myself, 'I bet I could learn to play that thing,' so I went over to his house later and asked him to show me what he knew. But they didn't even tune the guitar like they tune it today. They tuned to a natural chord, but I never heard anyone using a slide. I call it a pipe.

"At that time I hadn't heard many records, but after I learned to play guitar I left home. Didn't finish school after seventh grade, just thought I could get through the world and the rest was common sense. I told my mama maybe I could get a better job and send her some money back. I went to New Orleans and the first job I got was as a dishwasher at the Rosedale Hotel; my uncle knew a man working there and got them to give me a trial. You had to keep them dishes moving, work there from eight o'clock in the morning until four thirty with thirty minutes' break. You really had to scratch them dishes, but they didn't give you any gloves, so in wintertime when I came out of there, I'd have to put my hands in my pockets to keep them warm.

"At that time I didn't have much interest in playing music, but after I lost my job at the Rosedale Hotel I got a job at a gambling house as a porter. Then they went out of business and I found myself back in Donaldsonville, but I heard there was a lot of work going on out in

Texas. That winter I worked on a farm in Jeanerette, [near] New Iberia, worked and saved all the money I could. I met my oldest boys' mother there, Bertie Lee.

"She and I looked as though we were getting along pretty good, so I stayed there. After the summer I said I'd stay until the next winter, but she suggested I should go out to Texas. After I got there I was making five dollars an hour . . . digging out land for new pipes at the Gulf Oil Refinery; that was really good money then. That's how I got to meet Guitar Jr. I was living in Port Arthur with two old people in their house, and he suggested I went to live with him. We was both trying to learn to play guitar, so this seemed like a good idea."

In an interview with *Living Blues* magazine, Lonnie Brooks,[2] a.k.a. Guitar Jr., recalled how the two men got started. "I said we'd do it just like Long John [Hunter][3] and them do; they've got two guitars. Lonesome Sundown would take and lower the strings on his guitar, make it sound like a bass. So he come and we found a drummer, Fred Johnson. Lonesome Sundown was doing all the singing and we were doin' everything—Hank Williams, Little Richard, Fats Domino, Elvis Presley, zydeco. We played a country place called Port Neches between Port Arthur and Beaumont. Most of the people, when they would leave the clubs in the city, would go out there because they stayed open twenty-four hours if they wanted to."[4]

Sundown was happy with this arrangement. "We stayed together for a while and practiced, but I wasn't very good on lead guitar. And as he was faster than I was, that was why I played bass behind him. We played numbers like 'Honest I Do' by Jimmy Reed, that sort of stuff and just did it for fun; I never thought I could get into recording or anything like that. Around 1955 I met Philip Walker,[5] who was playing with Clifton Chenier[6] and His Zydeco Ramblers. Because I could sing better than he could, he asked Clifton if he could use another guitar player. Philip got back in touch and asked me to come on over and play at this club in Lake Charles."

After hearing Sundown perform at the Blue Moon Club, Chenier gave him the job. As part of Chenier's band, he was soon playing dates along the Gulf Coast and traveling as far as Chicago and Los Angeles.

"I hadn't heard zydeco music before," Sundown admitted, "because I had come up in a blues environment, and my ear was trained to blues.

Clifton lived in St. Landry Parish and that was where he was playing, until an old man called J. R. Fulbright got in touch from Los Angeles. He'd heard him and asked if he'd like to cut some records; his first was 'Hey, Tite Fille.' When I started playing with Cliff I was still living in Port Arthur and Cliff was playing around St. Landry Parish. I met my wife, Gloria, when I was over at Philip Walker's house; she had washed her hair and was driving around to dry it. Philip said, 'Hey, Gator'—he always called me that—'we got some babes out here!' So that's how I got married; couldn't cut loose. Came back to Opelousas and got my own band together."

Back in Louisiana and now a settled, married man, Sundown joined Lloyd Renauld's trio as singer and guitarist and began writing his own songs. Two of these he recorded on a demo tape.

"I played with Lloyd Renauld for a while but figured that if I could make it for him singing, then I could do it for myself. I started playing around Opelousas—Jimmy Reed and Fats Domino were my favorite singers—and Leroy Washington, who was a good friend of mine, taught me a whole lot of guitar I didn't know. I also taught Rudolph Richard to play; would share with him what I'd learned from Leroy. Then when Slim Harpo needed a guitar player, I introduced him to Rudolph, and Slim took Rudolph back to Baton Rouge. I had to get a second guitar player, so I hired a guy called Alvin Thomas; he didn't play very well but I figured I could suffer with it until I found someone better." He laughed. "I taught Rudolph's brother to play as well—we called him 'Lefty.' That boy would take his Gibson guitar and amplifier [and] walk three miles to my house, so I knew he was serious! He's one hell of a guitar player now and living down in Texas—Joseph Richard.

"When I first started recording I went through Jay Miller; I'd been to his studio with Katie Webster, who'd asked me to make some records with her. Two or three weeks later I was up in Opelousas, where my wife's mother lived, and she needed some air putting in her car tires. I went down to the filling station; there was J. D. Miller. So I went up and introduced myself. He said, 'Yeah—I remember you. You played guitar.' I said, 'Mr. Miller, if it's possible I'd sure like to come on down and record some numbers.'

"He said, 'Sure, that's no problem. Get your guitar and come down to the studio and I'll listen to what you got.' So I got my group together—I had a three-piece band at the time with Lloyd Renauld on drums, Talton Miller on piano, and another guitarist who played behind me— and went right on over. It looked like a record store, radio-repair shop, and studio combined; you couldn't tell which was which! But right away when he heard the song I'd written, 'Lost Without Love,' he said, 'That's it. I'll record it.'"

Sundown's reverb-drenched guitar riff owed much to Muddy Waters' "Still a Fool," but the background piano arpeggios and intriguing lyrics lifted the song into another dimension. "I was thinking about a bird when I wrote that song; if he hasn't got any feathers he can't fly, and a man without a woman, he can't get up!" Sundown said with a laugh.

Jay Miller also came up with a new name for Cornelius Green. When the tapes of the gloomy "Lost Without Love" were mailed to Nashville, it was as Lonesome Sundown that his voice would hit the airwaves. "When I went home and told my wife and mother-in-law about it, they said, 'We'll see what happens.' My wife's mother was a schoolteacher and she told me a lot of funny stuff that I'd write down so I could remember it; that way I could maybe use it in another song," Sundown added with a smile.

"About a month and a half later, they were saying on the radio that they had this new artist, Lonesome Sundown, and when I heard that, I was so excited I woke my mother-in-law up in her bed!" But his euphoria was short lived.

"The way Miller explained it to me, I would be recording for him but the records would come out of Nashville. So because I was contracted to him, it meant that I was also contracted to Nashville. But I had no knowledge of the business, . . . and that's why I didn't think Miller treated me right. I originally got paid $400, but apart from a couple of times when he helped out for my band to travel places, that's all I can ever remember getting paid.

"When we had records out, we got hired more frequently, and there was a lot of good little groups around Opelousas."

In 1961, Jay Miller arranged for Sundown and several other Excello artists to play some showcase dates in Chicago. For their transportation, he took special delivery of the first VW van to enter Louisiana, the musicians driving the six hundred or so miles up Highway 61 to the Windy City. But the trip was far from a success. Inexplicably, rather than play their own songs, Lazy Lester, Slim Harpo, and Katie Webster performed hits by B. B. King and Bobby Bland. The foray North was a disaster and not one that was repeated.

"There must have been six or eight of us and we were like a bunch of sardines in a can!" Sundown snorted. Relegated to gigs nearer to home, for many of the Excello artists, LSU with its fraternity houses was a lucrative source of work.

"Slim Harpo was one of the first people to book me over in LSU, but generally we never moved away too much to play because we were ripped off. LSU was still segregated at the time, but the people in Louisiana believed in getting along with one another. Segregation set back the income of black bands, and because black folks didn't have the money, they'd throw their own little house parties, because they were afraid to go places where blacks and whites would mix."

I felt sad that after all these years Sundown, a good-natured man, still harbored dark thoughts about his experiences in Crowley. "When he [Miller] started, he didn't have anything. The artists are the ones that built his business—myself, Lightnin' Slim, Slim Harpo, Katie Webster—we put him on the road."

Despite his reservations, Sundown continued to work with Jay Miller into the early 1960s. His 1964 "Hoo Doo Woman Blues" and "I've Got a Broken Heart" recordings have been described as among "the last ethnic down-home blues 45's aimed exclusively at the Negro market." Another early standout track from his time at Excello, a loping blues widely covered by artists including Slim Harpo and later Ronnie Earle and the Broadcasters, was "My Home Is a Prison" (1957). The song was apparently made up on the spot in the studio, inspired by Sundown's wife telephoning and asking him to come home!

As I got up to leave, begrudgingly Sundown did admit that his viewpoint was not one shared by everyone.

"Lightnin' Slim got along with Miller, but he must have had some agreement different from mine. Lazy Lester got on with him all right as well, but he was always on the jolly side and he could blow that harmonica, blew on some of my records. I hate to think that we got people like Miller down in Louisiana, though. One of the Ten Commandments is 'thou shalt not steal.' I was sergeant at arms in the church and because of them, I stopped playing blues. I learned that

God made us for his purpose, and I believe it was wrong to be playing blues when he needed us. He said everything should be done in the name of Jesus Christ, and you wouldn't play the blues in the name of Jesus Christ. Anything that isn't right I believe is devilish, and you have an obligation to God to do what he wants."

After a messy divorce, Sundown walked away from music and was ordained as a minister in the Apostolic Church. "Blues is something that's for the joy of man, not God. Most of the time you can't find joy in it, but I started playing because I heard my father, and I liked it more than other stuff," he reflected.

Then in 1977, Sundown had a change of heart, restrung his Telecaster guitar, and recorded a comeback album, *Been Gone Too Long*. Produced by Bruce Bromberg and Dennis Walker, with Philip Walker adding backup guitar, the album was recorded for Joliet Records and released by Alligator Records and later HighTone.

With Sundown handling soulful songs such as "Breaking Up Somebody's Home," the jaunty, rocking "Louisiana Lover Man," and down-home blues songs such as "If You Ain't Been to Houston," this was one of his finest hours. But despite the promotion of these two larger companies, the album sank without trace. It was his last throw of the dice.

In 1994, Sundown suffered another stroke and was left unable to speak. He passed away on April 23, 1995, in Gonzales, where he is buried. A huge talent, in 2000 he was inducted into the Louisiana Blues Hall of Fame.

Tabby Thomas, 1979 (Author's Collection)

Chapter Seven

Tabby Thomas, King of the Swamp Blues

In 1987, talking about Baton Rouge blues inevitably meant talking about "Rockin' Tabby Thomas." Everyone had heard of the self-styled "King of the Swamp Blues"—club owner, guitarist, pianist, and singer. That's not to say that they had all hung out at the Blues Box drinking Jack Daniel's, but most knew about the joint. It was legendary.

And few would deny that as the proud, genial proprietor of Baton Rouge's number-one blues club, he was the finest ambassador the city had. Tabby led a relentless, one-man blues crusade, especially for the homeboys such as Silas Hogan and Guitar Kelly. He loved to have his efforts acknowledged—he was particularly proud of a Lifetime Achievement Award from the South Louisiana Music Association— but was equally pleased to see his peers receive recognition. After his passing in January 2014, his absence remains a huge loss to the music community, and his legacy isn't likely to fade away any time soon.

Tabby was something of a musical anachronism. Gifted with a rich, sonorous voice, on the one hand he was influenced by West Coast bluesmen Roy Brown, Amos Milburn, and Charles Brown. But he also loved the music of Lightnin' Slim, Whispering Smith, Slim Harpo, and, of course, Silas Hogan and Guitar Kelly. Theirs was real down-in-the-alley, gutbucket blues, gestated during the early hours in small country jukes.

Born on Myrtle Street in Baton Rouge on January 5, 1929, just six blocks away from where the Blues Box stood, Tabby recalled how the city was served only by radio station WJBO.

"It was a white station, which used to play all kinds of records. Gene Autry, Frank Sinatra, Jimmie Davis . . . but I used to love the cowboys. At the same time, . . . I was going to church and hearing the choir singing. My aunt Tish was a soloist at the church; she used to make 'em shout and fall out." He laughed. "All my family were in the church; my grandfather owned the church that he founded—the Seventh Day Baptist church," he remembered.

"My mother used to . . . have all kinds of blues records—she's a strict Christian now—but that's how I heard all those blues records. I used to love to listen to that Peetie Wheatstraw, 'The Devil's Son-in-Law,' and Son House. Big Boy Crudup, Tampa Red—my mother used to have all them records. We used to go to a little place called Butlers Drug Store, where we drank Cokes and stuff. They had a jukebox in there and that's when I first started listening to Big Joe Turner. He had this record, 'My Daddy Was a Jockey and He Taught Me How to Ride.' And when I heard that Joe Liggins record 'The Honeydripper'—boy, I'd be jitterbuggin'! That's when I started keeping up with the records, because they didn't have no black radio station. The only time that you heard black records was on the jukebox. You might get to hear Louis Jordan, the Ink Spots, or Duke Ellington on the white stations, but that was about it."

During the late 1930s and early '40s, the suburbs of Baton Rouge became increasingly industrialized. But people still thought of it as a "country town," a place far removed from the cosmopolitan atmosphere of New Orleans.

And it was also strictly segregated. "You just grew up with it—accepted it. Like you grew up with the electric light. Turn it on—you know that it's going to work. That's what it was like. You had to sit at the back of the bus always. Might have been hot as hell back there over the engine—especially in the summer—but even if there wasn't one person on that bus, you didn't sit up front where the white folks sat. I never felt bad about it though, never lost my pride.

"OK—say I go sit where the white folks sit. The policeman comes, busts me upside my head, and pushes me in jail. What did I want to do that for? You just accept it. It's just like you had a white water fountain there, and a black water fountain over there. *You* had to go to the black fountain. The water in the white fountain was cold, the water in the black fountain hot! If you wanted a hamburger, *you* couldn't go to the front. You had to go to the side and go to the back and pay for it! Pay your damn money and eat your sandwich. You couldn't sit down and eat it!" He laughed.

"If you wanted to take a leak, you had to go down to the levee somewhere. You couldn't go to where the white folks was goin'; you had to go somewhere else! That's just the way it was."

The North Boulevard that Tabby Thomas knew as a child was far removed from the stretch of urban decay it had become by 1987. On weekends it was buzzing with life, and in an era before cars were an everyday necessity, Tabby remembers it being packed with couples, walking home late at night from the downtown clubs. Now demolished, the tall building that stood opposite the "Box" was the Temple Roof Garden, a Masonic Hall and barbershop and for almost forty years the hub of the city's music scene. A venue for prime U.S. jazz acts, it quickly become the hottest gig in town, featuring the talents of stars such as Count Basie and Duke Ellington, along with R&B chart acts.

Baton Rouge was a "Monday-night town." Acts passing through the South would play the Temple Roof Garden on a Monday night, often for a fraction of their fee, merely to obtain a gig on a slack night of the week. By all accounts the gig was a popular one, too.

Sam Johnson was involved with the local Odd Fellows group, which was headquartered at the Temple Roof. Under his enthusiastic leadership, a succession of big-time show bands visited the town, with profits from the gigs being plowed back into the community via various Odd Fellows programs.

"Man, you'd have them hanging off the roof to get a look!" Tabby recalled with a laugh. "Those guys wouldn't have to buy no liquor or anything when they was in town; those bands would rather come to Baton Rouge than to New Orleans. There you'd have cats gettin' rough, gettin' loose—all kinds of ways. Here they was *loved*, man!"

But in the segregated days of the South, the audience, lindy-hopping or swinging out to the likes of Cab Calloway and Louis Armstrong, was always 100 percent black. This state of affairs would continue until the 1960s.

Just as the Temple Roof Garden was packing them in, Tabby left town to join the air force. "The air force had just got integrated when I arrived, and I was put in a mixed squadron, where we all ate together and played together. After Baton Rouge it did seem quite strange, but there were never any problems. I did my basic training in San Antonio, and then I was stationed up at McChord Air Force Base in Washington State.

"After that, I volunteered to go to Guam and got the chance to go to Tokyo and Yokohama in Japan. What was strange then was that although the air force was integrated at home, it wasn't integrated overseas; they had a black outfit, and they had a white outfit. I personally didn't have any race problems, but I *did* have problems with the first sergeant!

"I used to play cards, shoot dice, that sort of thing. So one day I was playing in a game where a lot of guys lost their money. They complained to the commanding officer, Major Seaton. Now this guy didn't like blacks anyway, and when he heard what had happened, he had me put up for a court martial. As it happened I only had another thirty days to go; my time was up. This Major Seaton was so anxious to get me that he didn't get to find this out. By the time that he had organized the court martial, it was too late. There was nothing that he could do!"

After leaving the air force, Tabby found himself on the West Coast, freed from the restrictions of service life. He smiled as he remembered how he "ran wild," admitting to "a lot of drinking, marijuana, and beach parties." During his time in the Pacific, Tabby had bought himself a saxophone. Although he was unable to make any real progress on the instrument, it nurtured in him the idea to eventually become a performer.

The San Francisco of the 1950s was an ideal place for an aspiring singer to be hanging out. Many of the leading R&B performers of the day—Roy Brown, Johnny Otis, T-Bone Walker, and Tabby's hero, Charles Brown—regarded the Golden State as home.

Inspired by seeing Lowell Fulson perform at the Primalon Ballroom, Tabby entered a local talent contest, singing Roy Brown's song "Long About Midnight." To his surprise he won, beating out a budding young singer called Johnny Mathis and also Etta James. Tabby heard that Hollywood Records were looking for new singers to record, and encouraged by his success, he eagerly sought them out.

"I went down to their studios and at first I was worried. At the same time that I was there, they had Little Caesar and Larry Williams both recording. I told them that I'd just won first prize in this talent contest, so this guy gives me this piece of paper—no music—and says, 'Sing that.'

"I looked at the words and started to sing 'Midnight Is Calling.' He immediately stopped me and said, 'That's it . . . let's cut it.' And that turned out to be my first record. I'd done all this on my lunch hour, so when I got back and told my boss that I had made a record, he said, 'What? If you're gonna be a star, then I want to be your manager!'

"Two weeks later the record came out on Hollywood Records, and they were playing the hell out of it all over California. The band on that record was led by a guy called Que Martin—a hell of a musician; I later heard he went on to play with T-Bone Walker."

The boss of Hollywood Records was John Dolphin, a large light-skinned man from Detroit who liked to be called "Big John." Until his untimely death on New Year's Day in 1959—Dolphin was shot in front of Beach Boy Bruce Johnston by a songwriter to whom he allegedly owed money—his artists included Sam Cooke, Charlie Mingus, and Pee Wee Crayton.

But like many record producers at the time, reputedly John Dolphin wasn't keen on paying royalties. What his artists received instead was unlimited airplay on radio stations such as WKRD and KGFJ, broadcasting Dolphin-sponsored shows designed to promote his product.

The downside of this continuous airtime was that an artist like Tabby could easily be hoodwinked into imagining his records were more popular than they actually were. However, exposure on other stations might be nonexistent.

Just how popular Tabby's record became, he never really found out. After he'd been in California for six months, he ran into what, in true bluesman tradition, he described as some "bad luck."

"I got a girl pregnant, and her mother was chasin' me around, wantin' to put me in jail." He laughed. "Eventually they caught up with me, and I wound up being put in jail. While I was in there I thought, 'Hell, I'm going home. . . .' I was only twenty-one at the time and they put me in jail because the girl was seventeen. California's a bad place to get a [young] girl pregnant—they put your ass in jail quick!"

Tabby related how he caught a Greyhound bus back to New Orleans to find that the B side of his record, an up-tempo shuffle called "I'll Make the Trip," was now the theme song for a show by the legendary Okie Dokie, one of the Crescent City's hottest DJs. At the radio station,

Tabby introduced himself to the surprised receptionist and, as the singer of Okie Dokie's theme song, asked to go on the show. By the time he got back to Baton Rouge the next day, it seemed as though the whole world was waiting for him.

But after the initial excitement had died down, Tabby found that there was little work to be had in the town. Unable to play any instrument at this point, he was eventually hired as a singer by local bandleader Eddie Shaw. As featured vocalist with the group, he toured much of Louisiana, meeting Clifton Chenier for the first time.

Late in 1954, when the band was playing in New Orleans, Tabby also became friendly with a short, wiry guitarist called Eddie Jones, who performed under the stage name of Guitar Slim. Although Slim had no records to his credit, he was gaining a sizable local reputation for his startling stage shows. Slim would dye his hair in frightening colors and, aided by a monster guitar cable, ride out into the street on the shoulders of an audience member, an unheard-of gimmick at the time. Although not a technically proficient guitarist, Slim had developed a unique style, relying on distorted notes played through the speakers of the PA system rather than a backline amplifier, and using controlled feedback. He was a killer and the crowds loved him.

"When I was in California, someone heard me singing and told Art Rupe,[1] who was the owner of Specialty Records, that he should check me out. Art Rupe flew down to New Orleans while I was there and asked to hear some songs. At the time I didn't have any original material, but when I had my stuff together, I called up Johnny Vincent,[2] who worked with Art Rupe and was recording Little Richard.

"He came out to my mother's house and said, 'Tabby, I want you to hear something.' The demo record that he played me was 'The Things That I Used to Do.' He wanted me to record it, but I said that it just wasn't my style; somehow I just couldn't see myself singing it."

Two months later the record became a monster hit, selling over a million copies and making Guitar Slim a legend almost overnight.

Undaunted by this piece of bad luck, and noticing the popularity of Fats Domino, Tabby decided to learn to play piano.

"The first thing that I had was just a sheet of cardboard with the keys marked out! Huey Smith would come by sometimes and show me how to finger the chord shapes. Then I'd sit down with the piece of cardboard and try to get the shapes into my head. When I finally did manage to get a piano, I didn't have much else—just a piano and a bed in the whole house!"

At this time, Fats Domino[3] still played most of the major nightspots in Louisiana, and Tabby recalled their first meeting.

"Fats was playing over the road at the Temple Roof one Monday night, and I'd got to the gig early and met Fats in the dressing room. He asked me if I'd come over here—the Box was a drugstore in those days—and get him a pint of gin. By the time that I got back, Fats was talking to Dave Bartholomew and he wasn't happy! He said, 'Man— I'm tired. I just wanna go home and see my wife.' At this time he had just had a big hit with 'Ain't That a Shame.' Anyway, he got Dave Bartholomew to phone up his agent in Chicago. That man just said, 'Godd----—I got him hot and now he can keep his ass out there until I tell him to come in!' Well, they kept him out there and eventually that made him. When you're hot, you just gotta stay out there."

For a family man, "staying out there" could never be as easy as it sounded. For Tabby, like many local bluesmen, the security of his family came first. He had seen too many others fall by the wayside, including his friend Huey Smith. Once living in style in a New Orleans lakeside house, Huey ended up in a government housing project when his money ran out.

Soul man Joe Tex was also a regular performer around town. "I remember seeing Joe Tex come to play at the Apex club right here in town, and when he stepped out of the car, all he had with him was a small brown suitcase. Few years later, he had all those million sellers and in the end he passed away. There's so many of those guys in the graveyard that I think, 'S---, if I've got to die to have a hit record, then I don't need no hit records!" He laughed. "I'd rather stay out here for another twenty years poor!"

With the emergence of the civil rights movement, the 1950s were turbulent times in the South, and as Tabby recalled, Baton Rouge was no exception. "There used to be this drive-in called Harper's Drive-in. This white lady that owned it had a daughter who'd been in a big film out in Hollywood called *The Mississippi Gambler*. Now this wasn't too long after I'd come back from California and I was friendly with Buddy Stewart, who at the time was singing with the George Williams band. Buddy said, 'Look, man, Miss Harper's having a party. Why don't you come?'

"Now this Miss Harper had both blacks and whites working for her. A black cook, a white manager, black waiters—she was a kind woman. Anyway, we went up there and it was a really fine party. There was a band up there, a comedian, and everybody was having a pretty good time. Now because this place was a diner, it had a big glass window out front, and everyone passing could look in and see what was going on, see the people dancing.

"Well, there was white guys dancing with black girls, black guys dancing with white girls; everybody was just havin' a good time. Suddenly there was a knock at the door and there was the chief of police with about twenty-five state troopers. Man, his face was red. He was cryin' with rage! He said, 'Miss Harper, godd--- it—what's going on in there? What are them niggers doing with those white girls in there? If you don't get those niggers out of the place, I'm going to blow it down. I swear to God!' Now when all this started I didn't know what to do. I'd been out in California, where we didn't have to put up with this s---! There was a lawyer there and he went up to the police chief and gave him a sign—a Masonic sign. The police chief just looked at him mad and said, 'I don't know that godd--- sign you're giving me. We're going to go in and get those niggers!'

"I saw a friend of mine and said, 'Man, I'm gonna check you later!' and I crept out of the place out of the back. Practically the next day the Louisiana legislature went into session and passed a law saying that black and white couldn't fraternize or congregate together. In my opinion that was one of the things that ignited the civil rights movement in Baton Rouge."

The fifties witnessed a hardening of white attitudes towards blacks, and throughout the South, the segregation that Tabby had come to accept as part of his daily life was being openly challenged. In Baton Rouge, where blacks and whites both rode the buses together, the transport system became one of the first arenas in the fight against segregation. In 1953, the black community successfully petitioned the city council to pass an ordinance allowing blacks to choose bus seats on a first-come, first-served basis.

Although blacks would still have to sit at the back of the bus over the engine, no seats would any longer be reserved for whites. When the back was full, black passengers could use the seats previously reserved for whites. However, the white bus drivers saw fit to ignore the city council ruling and continued to reserve seats for their white passengers. In an attempt to force compliance with the order, the black community staged a one-day boycott of the city's buses.

Ironically, by the end of the successful boycott, the Louisiana attorney general declared the new city council ruling illegal and stated that the bus drivers didn't need to follow it. But three months later, a weeklong bus boycott led by the Reverend T. J. Jemison finally induced the city council to reach an acceptable compromise. Two seats would be reserved for whites at the front and one long seat at the back for blacks. Compared to subsequent civil rights triumphs, the Baton Rouge one was minor, but it did pave the way for the much larger action that later took place in Montgomery, Alabama.

Tabby's first recording session happened around this time. With local bandleader Buddy Stewart in tow, later the proprietor of Buddy's Rock Shop on North Acadian, and several members of Stewart's band with whom he'd been working, he made the journey to Jackson, Mississippi, home of Trumpet Records.

The first Mississippi-based company to achieve national stature through its distribution, sales, radio airplay, and promotion, the label had started almost by accident. In 1949, Willard and Lillian McMurry purchased a hardware store on 309 North Farrish Street, with an inventory that included a stack of blues and rhythm and blues 78s. Sensing the demand for the music, the McMurrys built a makeshift recording studio in the back of the store and, in an inspired move, recorded Sonny Boy Williamson II and Elmore James.

In 1952, Elmore James' "Dust My Broom" achieved spectacular success, rising to the second spot on the *Billboard* rhythm and blues chart, a fact that hadn't escaped Tabby's notice.

Possibly surprised by Tabby's big-band approach, a far cry from the simpler Mississippi blues she was used to recording, Lillian McMurry suggested that he look elsewhere. Overhearing the conversation, one of the studio engineers, Jimmie Ammons, invited the group to call at his small home studio. Anxious not to return to Baton Rouge emptyhanded, they set up in Ammons' primitive studio, which Tabby recalled being in the kitchen, and recorded "Church Members Ball," a jumping piece of jive in the Big Joe Turner tradition. The record—attributed to "Tabby Thomas and His Mellow Mellow Men"—was issued on the Delta Records label. Sadly, it failed to make any impact but did re-establish Tabby's local credibility as a recording artist.

Slim Harpo, who by this time was doing good business for Excello Records, suggested to Jay Miller that he should record his friend. Tabby was still purely a singer—the piano and guitar playing would come later—and so when he drove to Crowley one Sunday afternoon, he took a band led by Bob Johnson.

"I had got to know about Miller through Slim and the other guys, and I could see that it was doing them all some good. I met J. D. Miller and he played me this song that he'd written called 'Tomorrow.' I thought that it was a good song and I felt that I could handle it."

A leisurely paced ballad in the New Orleans style, the record fared well locally but failed to make any significant impression. However, Tabby's swamp-blues immortality was assured when he recorded his self-penned "Hoodoo Party," its popularity undoubtedly helped by the fact that the great DJ John R. played it to death on Nashville's WLAC.

Recorded in 1961 at Jay Miller's Crowley studio, with its stop-time format and voodoo imagery, "Hoodoo Party" is Willie Dixon's "Hoochie Coochie Man" transplanted to the Louisiana swamps. But there all similarity ends. With Katie Webster's rolling piano holding down the rhythm, and Lazy Lester's mournful harmonica solo, it becomes two minutes and twenty-four seconds of classic swamp blues.

Tabby later said that the idea for the song came about after he'd seen an item on local television about a meeting of voodoo practitioners in New Orleans. He subsequently visited the tomb of Marie Laveau, the famed voodoo queen, and "Hoodoo Party" was born.

Sadly Tabby failed to capitalize on the record's success, and there was no follow-up. And now social revolutions were dramatically changing musical tastes. Studios such as Stax and Muscle Shoals were coming up with high-voltage soul sounds, records that made the country blues of the Excello artists sound archaic. By the time America succumbed to the Beatles and Rolling Stones, the writing was on the wall, a fact not lost on J. D. Miller. In the mid-sixties, Excello ceased recording blues artists.

Left in creative limbo, Tabby during this period released many self-produced singles, on his Bluebeat label. They often mirrored current dance crazes, such as the up-tempo slice of funk, "Popeye Train"—now a rare piece of vinyl changing hands for over three hundred dollars. It's perhaps hard to come to terms with the fact that the singer exhorting his listeners to "get on down" is the very same man who recorded "Hoodoo Party."

"I never wanted to stay just in the blues bag," Tabby said with a laugh. "I've written things that's really not what you'd call blues."

Other releases included several fine soul records, cut with Ed Snead and Lionel Whitfield, who owned the local Whit label. But it wasn't until the beginning of the 1980s, with the release of his album entitled *25 Years with the Blues*, that Tabby's blues recording career enjoyed a renaissance.

Baton Rouge was experiencing something of a blues boom, sparked by Nick Spitzer, a blues enthusiast on the city's Arts and Humanities Council. It seemed that people had begun to wake up to the talent on their doorstep. For ten years, Tabby had been doing very little musically, but encouraged by this turn of events, he left his day job at a local chemical plant and eventually fulfilled his long-nurtured dream of opening a blues club.

"When I finally got that opening night, there was Henry Gray, Whispering Smith, Silas [Hogan], and Guitar Kelly. Man, you couldn't get in the place," Tabby remembered. (Pianist Henry Gray spent years playing and recording with Howlin' Wolf in Chicago, and Whispering Smith was the inseparable harmonica buddy of Lightnin' Slim. By my time in Baton Rouge, Whispering Smith had passed away, and Henry Gray was rarely seen at the Box.)

The club served as a valuable showcase for the Baton Rouge musicians, and European blues fans soon sought it out. It also functioned as the first venue where white and black music fans might safely mix; previously the only opportunity for white blues fans to catch the local bluesmen in action might have been the less than ideal settings of the LSU fraternity dances. Blues clubs in Baton Rouge,

The Arts and Humanities Council of Greater Baton Rouge

presents

A SATURDAY MORNING OF BLUES

with

HENRY GRAY   GUITAR KELLY

TABBY THOMAS   SILAS HOGAN

MOSES "WHISPERING" SMITH

SATURDAY, JUNE 14TH
9 A.M. — 12 NOON

Lawn of the East Feliciana Parish Courthouse in Clinton

FREE ADMISSION

From Baton Rouge, take Plank Road to Clinton. Turn left on Hwy. 10 to the Courthouse.

Co-sponsored by the Louisiana Division
of the Arts and the Clinton Bank and
Trust Company.

Flyer for Nick Spitzer concert, 1979 (Author's Collection)

Henry Gray at the Blues Box, 1997 (Author's Collection)

traditionally dangerous even for black people, had definitely been "no-go" areas for whites.

In 1979, Tabby made the first of many appearances at the New Orleans Jazz & Heritage Festival. His killer set, which featured Big Bo Melvin on guitar, was widely acclaimed, even if, as he recalled, it was a nerve-wracking experience. "Man, I thought that we had trouble there! I got down there with my band, got onstage, but for some reason my Fender amp wouldn't work. Now the thing had never let me down before, so why it had to choose then I don't know! The only thing that I could do, because they didn't seem to have another amp, was play the piano. I wasn't really ready for that, but as soon as I started out with 'What'd I Say,' the place just erupted! At the end they just wouldn't let us off—must have done four encores. When I came offstage, Allen Toussaint came up to me and started huggin' me because he was just so pleased to hear someone else up there playing in that New Orleans piano style."

Moses "Whispering" Smith, 1979 (Author's Collection)

Caught in action by some Dutch promoters, shortly afterwards, along with Silas Hogan, Guitar Kelly, and Henry Gray, Tabby appeared at festivals in Amsterdam and Utrecht. Upon his return home, enthused by his success in New Orleans and Jay Miller's eagerness to record him, he again took the long concrete I-10 highway to the Crowley studios. The resultant album, *25 Years with the Blues* on Miller's Blues Unlimited label, featured Moses "Whispering" Smith on harmonica and Lafayette's Buckwheat on piano. It was a jumping mix of Louisiana blues that proved Tabby Thomas meant business.

Three more albums followed. *Rockin' with the Blues* featured Tabby's regular band, the Mighty House Rockers, comprising Brian Bruce on harmonica, Joe Hunter on bass, and his two sons, Tammy and Chris, on drums and guitar. The band was augmented by Henry Gray, with Bill Samuel, a regular member of Clarence "Gatemouth" Brown's band, handling sax duties. Eight of the songs were originals, all tinged with Tabby's quirky lyrics. "Hot Seat Blues" tells the story of a convicted man on death row.

Hello, warden, open that window.
I ain't stopped breathin' yet, you know.

Tammy Thomas (Author's Collection)

Well, I'm going to the hot seat,
But I want a little fresh air before I go. . . .

"Welfare Blues" was modeled closely on similar versions of the same theme by Albert Collins and B. B. King.

When I first met you, darlin', you were standing in the welfare line.
You had holes in your shoes and the dresses you had weren't worth a
dime.
Well, I've given you my food stamps and all my money too.
If I catch you messin' round, I'm gonna put some hurt on you.[4]

Tabby's original song "Leave It Like It Is," a slow soul burn, is arguably one of his finest moments.

Rockin' with the Blues marked the beginning of Tabby's involvement with record man Floyd Soileau and his Maison de Soul label in Ville Platte. As you'd expect from a label based deep in the heart of Cajun territory, Soileau traditionally dealt mainly with country and Cajun music, and as his only blues artist, Tabby was justly proud.

For his next album, *Blues Train*, Tabby enlisted the help of the same musicians, with extra assistance from Oscar "Harpo" Davis on harmonica and Larry Garner on guitar. It was an intriguing mix, including standards such as Louis Jordan's "Caldonia" and Elmore James' "Can't Hold Out." Then in April 1988, Tabby released a follow-up album, *King of Swamp Blues.*

Recorded at Baton Rouge's Chimes Street Studios, the cover showed Tabby clutching a Gibson 335 guitar festooned with Spanish moss. I had the pleasure of coproducing and playing guitar on the disc, which also featured Oscar Davis on harmonica, Bill Samuel and Steve Hutter on saxes, and a rhythm section of drummer Barrie Edgar and bassist Doug Broussard. Once again, Tabby chose to record a wide variety of material, ranging from the rolling New Orleans style of "Jerri Dean" to out-and-out R&B, as on the rocking "I Love Big Fat Women."

A prolific writer of songs and a lyricist second to none, Tabby deserved to be far more widely recognized. Possibly, however, the very factors that made him special also worked against him. The blues was on a roll, but eighties audiences expected blues artists to conform

King of Swamp Blues *band, Baton Rouge, 1988* (Author's Collection)

to preordained stereotypes. Tabby was a singer able to handle a gutbucket blues as convincingly as a soul number, so some his music was hard to get a handle on. And he wasn't alone. Even Robert Cray, the big young hope of the blues world and a singer widely admired for his soul-inflected vocals and stinging guitar playing, came in for criticism from rigid blues fans.

For his part, Tabby happily embraced most styles of modern music that came along, even recording a hilarious rap track, "Killer Bees," with his son Chris Thomas King. The early nineties saw Tabby complete two very successful European tours with Junkyard Angels. He appeared at London shows organized by the U.K.'s Blues South West, alongside Buddy Guy, Junior Wells, and Joe Louis Walker and played some large venues and festivals where, to his delight, many European fans knew his old songs.

And in later years, Tabby at last seemed to obtain the local recognition that was his due. In 1998, I caught him playing at an open-air concert in downtown Baton Rouge, resplendent in an immaculate suit and white fedora. Admirers flocked around asking for autographs, as the King of the Swamp Blues beamed from ear to ear.

A larger-than-life character to the end, Tabby always hoped for that elusive hit record. But if "I Love Big Fat Women" never quite rivaled Michael Jackson in the charts, I'm not sure he really cared. And those of us fortunate enough to know him as a friend could only admire his tenacity and energy. He was always dedicated to his music and ready to help others along the path. Until a few years before he passed on January 1, 2014, just shy of his eighty-fifth birthday, new Tabby Thomas albums always seemed to be popping up in the record shelves. Sadly there will be no more.

Chapter Eight

Bruce Lamb, Neckbone Slim

"I would have been in hog heaven!"

Bruce Lamb

A guitarist who worshipped at the high altar of the Fabulous Thunderbirds and Anson and the Rockets, Bruce Lamb, a.k.a. Neckbone Slim, and his band the Circuit Breakers regularly worked with Silas Hogan and on the LSU gig circuit.

"I moved here in 1968 and there was a lot more going on then. That would have been about the time of the first great white blues revival in the States—John Mayall and Eric Clapton.[1] It started catching on, and I used to go across the river with a friend of mine to Bird's Satellite Lounge on Highway 190. We'd back the car under a tree so we were in the shadows, roll the windows down, have a bottle of wine, and smoke as we listened to the music. But we never went in—we were too scared!

"I don't know if we would have got hassled or not, but that way we got to hear people like B. B. King, Bobby Bland . . . they all used to play in that little place. B.B. King came through every three months or so in the early seventies; 'The Thrill Is Gone' was big then, but he still played in that little place that could only hold about 120 people.[2]

"Tabby's was the first place that white kids went to and he deserves credit for that, getting that racial interaction going and managing to get some gigs around town in the local white bars. At the time he'd just put out the album *25 Years with the Blues* and played places like Chief's. They had Albert King, Albert Collins come and play and used some of the local guys as well. It was an old bar that you couldn't cram more than 120 people into, used to pack it like sardines! He moved up to Perkins Road and had major acts; Muddy Waters played there three nights in a row. But he closed because he just couldn't pull enough people in to pay his bills.

"The best thing was the first time I ever played with Silas Hogan. He knew that I played blues because I'd run into him at a music store.

"On a Sunday night, Tabby used to have his jam session; that was before he lost his food license. At the time you used to have to have something to eat to be there, a hot dog or something.

"We had gone in there, a friend on harp and another guy on upright bass, and Woolfolk was playing drums. Silas and Kelly showed up, because they usually played Sunday nights, as I was playing one of Silas's tunes, 'Free-Hearted Man,' a song that had been on one of Bruce Bastin's Flyright[3] albums in England. Silas had completely forgotten that he'd recorded that song, forgotten the words and everything, but when I sang it, you could see a lightbulb go on inside his head! We finished playing and when we got down off the bandstand, he asked me, 'Where did you learn that song from?' So I told him. He said, 'I had completely forgotten that I did that . . . would you mind playing it again?' So we played it all through and ever since that day I could do no wrong. I would go there every Sunday and there'd be three of us playing guitar—me, Silas, and Kelly—with Joe Sander on upright bass, Cadillac on harp. A lot of fun.

"I used to go to Tabby's every Wednesday, but I couldn't stand the constant out-of-tune stuff, people refusing to tune up together—that's what got me! No matter how hard you try, when you're playing in chaos, you can't sound good.

"Silas and Kelly used to play every Saturday night for about twenty years at a place called Rogers Club in Clinton. They'd play until the last person had just about passed out on the floor—about four o'clock in the morning. They used to play a lot of places, but even for people like them, there's just not a market anymore. What black bars are going to hire Silas and Kelly?

"Maybe in those little country joints, where those old folks still want to hear that stuff; there're still quite a few of those places but you have to be careful. There's always one smart ass out to get you. The fraternity dances here used to be like *Animal House*. The whole point about fraternities in the South hiring black bands, crazy white kids would hire them for phenomenal amounts of money. This was at a time when they'd normally be working Joe's Chittlin' Shed or something for whatever someone would shove in a jar.

"So it was new plus a little bit taboo; make you wanna have sex in the streets! They'd hire these bands for a great lot of money but always make them wait at the end to get paid, make them stand outside in the rain.

"'You black folks need to be out of here now—you don't belong. Want a sandwich? You can't have one of those but we'll get you one out of the kitchen. Glass of water? You can't use that fountain over there.' That kinda stuff really went on.

"Silas told me once about doing one of those big fraternity dances with Lonesome Sundown, and two houses up the street Guitar Gable was playing. Imagine that. I would have been in hog heaven!"

Raful Neal at the Baton Rouge Blues Festival, 1997 (Author's Collection)

Chapter Nine

Raful Neal, the Family Man

The likeable patriarch of one of the two royal families of the Baton Rouge blues—the Thomas family, of course, share equal billing on this one—Raful Neal was a tall, chunky man with a ready smile and a permanent twinkle in his eyes. He was always welcoming, and to visit his home was, for a short time at least, to become an honorary member of the extended Neal clan. When once asked how many of his ten talented siblings were musicians, Kenny Neal, Raful's oldest child, replied, "The whole nine yards of 'em." So it seemed to be, and with most of them usually around during my time in Baton Rouge, Raful's extended pink wood-frame house invariably was—to use an English colloquialism—"like Paddington Station."

At the time, Ray Jr., a fine guitarist in the B. B. King mold who later went on to play with Bobby Bland, could often still be seen around town. Noel was away playing bass with Chicago bluesman James Cotton, Darnell held down the bass in Kenny's band with Larry Neal on drums, and young Frederick Neal was playing keyboards with Raful. The three sisters, Darlene, Charleen, and Jackie,[1] all sang, but at the time not professionally.

Raful was born on June 6, 1936, and after the death of his parents, he and his sister, Cora, were raised by an aunt and uncle on a tenant farm in Chamberlin, West Baton Rouge Parish. Like many of his generation, Raful must have had a tough life, with music a welcome relief from the daily grind. And the music came courtesy of WLAC, "the nighttime station for half the nation," as it called itself, broadcasting from "Music Row" in Nashville.

During the fifties, radio station WLAC became legendary, and you won't find any musician of Raful's generation who didn't tune in. "At the time, most of the music I heard came from John R. on WLAC out of Nashville," he recalled. "That's all we would listen to: John R., Hossman, and Gene Nobles. Those cats would play some good music, and each evening we kids would sit down at about eight o'clock and tune in. Sonny Boy Williamson, Jimmy McCracklin, Sonny Terry, and Brownie McGhee—you'd hear them all."

The station boasted four nighttime rhythm and blues shows hosted by Gene Nobles, John R. (John Richbourg), Herman Grizzard, and Bill "Hossman" (or simply "Hoss") Allen, and its place on the airwaves was unassailable. Thanks to WLAC's 50,000-watt clear-channel designation, the signal blasted black R&B sounds through much of the Eastern and Midwestern states and, crucially, to its target audience— the African-American listeners of the Deep South. The station chose sponsors designed to attract the African-American community: makers of haircare products such as Royal Crown Hair Pomade or chicken hatcheries, which packaged baby scrub roosters and other stock in large quantities for sale. The jockeys developed a reputation for colorfully pitching those products on air; some product slogans lent themselves to sexually suggestive double entendres, which only increased the announcers' popularity among teen listeners.

"And at the time, all you'd hear wherever you went was blues," Raful remembered. "Sometimes we'd take a little building, fix up a jukebox for teenagers, and blues was all we used to dance to, especially Little Walter and 'Boogie Chillen' by John Lee Hooker.

"When I started playing music, I had a guy called Ike Brown playing drums. He was a guy that loved good music but just couldn't play it! He tried drums, harmonica, singing—but it just wasn't in him. If he'd had a little music in him, he'd have been the best musician in the world. He played harmonica before I did, but when I finally got one, I wasn't too interested, until I saw Little Walter, and I began to start singing about the same time."

Born in Marksville, Louisiana, Little Walter had made his name in Chicago playing behind Muddy Waters. Described by the late Jimmy Rogers as a "little squirrel-faced boy," Walter started out playing amplified harmonica on Chicago's famed Maxwell Street. When he hooked up with Muddy Waters, the early records they made together would change the face of country blues. Songs such as "Country Boy," "She Moves Me," and "My Fault" became vehicles for Walter's amplified and highly echoed harmonica, as it wrapped itself around the vocals, combining the fast fluid lines of a saxophone with the chordal richness of an organ. It was a revolutionary sound, as ground-breaking as Jimi Hendrix's work and unlike anything else.

In 1952, Walter's record "Juke" became a smash hit on the Billboard R&B charts—the only harmonica instrumental to ever reach No. 1. He jumped ship when Muddy's band was in Shreveport, hightailed it back to Chicago, and soon hit the road with a crack band he called the Aces, with David and Louis Myers on guitars and Freddy Below on drums. The music Walter and the Aces played was up-tempo, jumping R&B that made some of his former employer's blues sound staid in comparison.

"I saw Little Walter at the Temple Garden around the time that he had 'Juke' out, which was a big hit," Raful recalled. "I never thought I'd see a man blow harmonica like that and with a band that was so good; his band was one of the best bands that ever came through town." He laughed. "I was used to seeing bands at the time that had maybe two or three horns, but Walter's band just had two guitars, drums, and harmonica. The sound was unbelievable; he used a very expensive mic that was unlike any I'd seen at that time.

"In the studio I believe he used to use those little nine-dollar Bullet[2] mics, but on the road he had this big chrome mic, on which you could adjust the sound. It was a very powerful mic for the time, and he had it going through an out-a-sight PA with two speakers set back. It was loud!

"After I saw Walter I said to myself, 'I'm going to learn to play like that.' When I first started out on harmonica, at a store in the country where I lived, you could buy a Marine Band harmonica for a dollar, but that was a lot of money back then. But I knew it was the same thing Walter played, because I'd asked him: a Marine Band with ten holes. But he also had a chromatic, which he called 'The Master.' I thought, 'God dog,' when I heard him play that."

The Temple Roof Garden, a four-story building opposite Tabby Thomas's Blues Box, was a legendary venue. "I almost thought B. B. King lived here at the time because I saw him so often! He'd always come through, along with T-Bone Walker, Lowell Fulson, Fats Domino, the Clovers, Bobby Bland, Little Junior Parker.

"Guitar Slim used to play there a lot; he'd always have a packed house and was an incredible performer and singer. He loved to clown—put the guitar behind his back or his head, play it between his legs. I've seen him drink a whole half-pint of Scotch on the bandstand, White Horse Scotch. But he began to look bad, and I believe that's what killed him."

The next time Little Walter and the Aces hit town, Raful and his band the Clouds, by which time also featured Buddy Guy, figured they were ready.

"We'd got pretty good. We had Buddy and Phil Guy both in the band, with Charles Cross playing drums. We was hot! Buddy Guy came here from Torus, Louisiana up on the other side of New Roads, where he was playing with a guy called Big Poppa. I went out one Tuesday night and everybody was talking about the guitar player. 'Man, they got a little cat from out in the country, got him out of the cotton fields.' I went up there and it was like they said. He [Buddy] was a playin' son of a gun!

"I guess Buddy must have been about nineteen at the time. I followed him around and finally formed my own band, with Lazy Lester my first guitar player. He wasn't the best but at least he was there!

"But I had to get rid of Lester. Some guitar players can play the same thing but can't go no further, and that was Lester. I had to play this contest with Big Poppa and the Canecutters, and there wasn't anyone that could beat Big Poppa's band! He had another guitar player from Opelousas called Charlie—he was dangerous; he was bad.

"People said I was good on the harmonica, but I really ought to brush up on the guitar front: Lester just couldn't cut it. Got to the point where I must have fired Lester because I wanted to get into the big time! Luckily Buddy and Big Poppa had some kind of falling out, and I managed to get Buddy [Guy] to play in my band. We got really tight playing all these little joints; at Buddy's hometown in a joint called the Rockhouse, they'd be like flies climbing up the wall. The next time we had a showdown with Big Poppa, I won!

"So we all went over to where Little Walter was playing, a place called the Purple Circle Club, and thought, 'Let's cut his head'—we thought we was bad! Charles was dangerous on those drums, and Buddy Guy was a fast young guitar player by that time.

"The DJ asked Little Walter if we could get up; told him we were gonna cut his head. That scared me so I tried to get out, told Walter that I didn't have any harmonicas. He said, 'That's OK—I've got seven up there on the piano. You can blow any one you like.' We got up there but didn't know what to kick off with, so we started a fast number and we got the whole place rocking.

"I think they [Walter's band] might have been offended when they saw us going down with the crowd, and after we'd played four numbers they went back on, and man they put the heat on us! We felt like turning into roaches and crawling back outta there. That man played some stuff on the harmonica I could never have dreamed of."

Raful had struck up a friendship with Aces drummer Freddy Below[3] and, after the band left town, was surprised to receive a letter from him.

"Freddy Below kept writing, telling us to go up to Chicago. Buddy said, 'Great, man, let's you and I go up to Chicago.' But I told him I was planning to get married. 'You can still go and send back for your wife,' he said. But my mama didn't want me to go. I already had one kid—Kenny—and my wife was pregnant with another. Money was scarce; we weren't making more than six or seven dollars a night then. When we got thirty-five dollars for a gig, we was in the big league!

"Buddy said, 'C'mon, I want you to take me down to the pawnshop and get me a good-size suitcase.' And he was gone. I still think I did the best thing. Had I gone with Buddy to Chicago, I wouldn't have had a family, and there's no telling what might have happened!" He laughed. "It just wasn't for me to go, I guess. But I still have a little fun. Ain't got no money but have enough to live decent, and I'm still playing."

Raful and Freddy Below lost contact, and the next time Walter came through town, his drummer was Odie Payne. In 1959, Raful made his recording debut, with a cover of Katie Webster's "On the Sunny Side of Love," for Don Robey's Peacock label. Evelyn Johnson once said of her colorful business partner, "Robey didn't know a record from a hubcap." Nonetheless, Robey had built up an impressive roster of stars that included Clarence "Gatemouth" Brown, Bobby Bland, and Big Mama Thornton.

The record was recorded with Junior Parker's band.[4] "I went to Houston to see Junior Parker and Bobby Bland play at Robey's Bronze

Peacock Club," Raful recalled. "Had bought myself a Rocket 88, an Oldsmobile, and was doing good; I was playing eight nights a week and there ain't but seven!"

The record might have led to some serious success for Raful and his band but, due to a copyright dispute, was never released. "I used to play all through the week, ten o'clock Saturday morning—ten till two—and after that I'd leave to play Washington's Barn in Scotlandville, four o'clock until eight. Then I'd leave to play Cliff's Streamline Club in Port Allen, where we had a residency, set up for ten o'clock. I'd have a two-hour break but I wouldn't sleep or nuthin'—I wasn't tired. Then I'd play ten till two, drive all the way back to Baton Rouge, take Philip Guy back—Buddy was gone by then—drive all the way back across the river to Erwinville, which is about fifteen miles. I wonder now how I did it! From the start to the intermission I'd be blowing all the time, play on every song. That was when people were really enjoying the blues, and I guess that's what kept me going. When Jimmy Reed's records were coming out, I could play his sound right on tap; Little Walter's too. Man, I had it! I was making good money—not big money, but regular money, enough to live off.

"I played full time from 1955. Had a three-piece combo, no bass guitar. Every now and then I'd hire a second guitar, but they tended to mess up. But there was one guy called George who played with Big Poppa, and he could play good second guitar, play the bass parts and be right there with you. Jimmy Anderson used to come on my bandstand and play some numbers but I don't know what's happened to him."

As for cutting records, Raful Neal appears to have been dogged by bad luck. Prior to the abortive Don Robey session, he tried to set something up with J. D. Miller in Crowley.

"I went down to his [J. D. Miller's] studio, but the way he talked, he'd ask you to make a record, as long as you didn't ask no questions about how the royalties worked.

"I asked him about that one time and he got real nasty, told me that all I'd get was some good publicity. Jimmy Anderson, Lazy Lester, Silas [Hogan]—they were all happy with that; all they wanted was to get a record out. I wasn't no expert, but he started telling me that my timing was bad. We recorded a song, 'I Gotta Leave This Town,' but he never released it.

"Slim Harpo was the only one that ever got any money, $25,000 that he got from Excello in Nashville, but if it hadn't been for the people in Nashville, he would never have got it. Slim and I were good friends; he was a real nice guy. One time my car broke down and I was due to play in Shreveport, so he told me to come on over and borrow his car and trailer. I'd lend him money and he'd always pay me back, but sometimes if I was short I wouldn't ask him. He'd get mad and tell me, 'Take it; take it.' At the time I was getting more work around town than Slim. It wasn't until he started getting some success with his records that he started getting better money. But Slim used to have me over to his house, and when Kenny Ray was young, he'd stop by and we'd play harmonica together.

"He always wanted to make that big time, and he wanted to be a guitar player, but he could never have made it. He did love that guitar, though, and he used to play it in later years. He had Rudolph Richard from Opelousas in his band, and Opelousas had some bad guitar players! When Slim got his money, he bought a Cadillac, built him a nice house; $25,000 was a lot of money back then. A Cadillac was only about $7,000 new and his house would have been $14,000."

Over the years, Raful became established on the Southern blues circuit, visited Europe, and from time to time opened at clubs around town such as the Turning Point. Sunday nights he'd often be found playing the Curtis Lounge in Port Allen, close to where he'd lived before moving into Baton Rouge. "Now I just like to travel and play on weekends, maybe get home after and not be too far away," he told me at the time. "I'd like to get back into it full time, see Kenny and I go traveling, but I'd go at it a different way from the way I used to—make sure I got some rest!"

In 1987, Raful Neal did finally make it to album status. For those of us who'd heard him in action, the fact that it had taken so long seemed almost criminal.

Louisiana Legend was released by Bob Greenlee's Florida-based King Snake label, with son Kenny Neal on hand playing guitar. The album was a stomping slice of swamp blues, mixing covers "Honest I Do," "Steal Away," and "No Cuttin' Loose" and Raful's own songs, with the steaming "Luberta"—long a mainstay of his live sets—being a standout. The album was picked up by the Chicago-based Alligator Records in 1990. *I Been Mistreated* was released on Ichiban Records

The Curtis Lounge, Port Allen, 1987 (Author's Collection)

the following year, and in 1997 Raful contributed harmonica on Tab Benoit's album *Swampland Jam*.

Raful's last recording in 2001 was aptly titled *The Hoodoo Kings*, an album that saw him sharing the honors with Rockin' Tabby Thomas and pianist Eddie Bo. Raful passed away on September 1, 2004, a huge loss to the blues community.

Chapter Ten

The Twenty-First-Century Bluesman

Mercurial, enigmatic, talented—it's easy to run out of superlatives when describing Chris Thomas King. The first time I ran into Chris, he was sitting quietly in the Blues Box. Dressed in an immaculate suit and his hair cropped short, he was about to set off with his band to play a high-school prom. Since that time in 1987, his career has experienced more twists and turns than the Mississippi River south of Vicksburg. But then anyone who includes Prince, Jimi Hendrix, and Bob Marley among their formative influences, only to spend the next few years hammering out gutbucket blues in their father's blues club, is inevitably going to have something of an identity crisis.

But ironically, due to spending almost two decades singing the

Chris Thomas King, early 1980s (Author's Collection)

blues for real, Chris finally achieved a major breakthrough. In the 2001 Coen brothers movie *O Brother, Where Art Thou?*, he played the part of thirties bluesman Tommy Johnson, a man who supposedly sold his soul to the devil. Leaving aside the phenomenal success of the film— the soundtrack alone sold 7.9 million copies—it allowed Chris artistic breathing space, setting him off on a track that shows no sign of an end. You never quite know what he's going to get up to next.

Born in 1962, Chris says he began playing the guitar when he was nine years old, but it's easy to imagine him strumming a twelve bar in E when barely out of diapers. Playing at the Blues Box as a young teen alongside guys such as Whispering Smith, Silas Hogan, and Guitar Kelly, often from six o'clock in the evening until three o'clock in the morning, he couldn't help but graduate summa cum laude in down-home Louisiana swamp blues.

"In my dad's club, it was like if the piano player didn't show up, 'hey, get on the piano!' Because we were playing for our supper—a family business—and the show must go on. So you gotta play the drums, mop the floor, take the cans out when the club closes, go sell the cans the next morning, put the cans in this bag and the bottles in that one . . . the whole thing as far as running a bar, the whole juke-joint experience!

"My dad pretty much operated his business out of a cigar box. You got a cigar box right here and you have a .45 right next to it. All this stuff about you should have a cash register and networking, he didn't know nothing about all that. A cigar box and a .45 right next to it—that's how he did business. So here I am, I'm a teenager and some nights when he wasn't there, I'd go and open up. And he'd tell me, make sure I go in the club with the .45 in my hand—don't have it in your pocket; have it in your hand—and have the key in the other hand with the money bag, so that people know you're prepared. You go in the club like that and at the end of the night, you get the money bag and everything for the following day. You put the .45 in your hand, keys in the other hand, lock the club, and leave like that. That was my introduction to the music business."

However, Tabby Thomas often related how he and Chris fought like cats and dogs about music. As they are both fiercely opinionated, it's easy to imagine the sparks that must have flown in the Thomas household when these two discussed the relative merits of Led Zeppelin and Fats Domino!

Interviewed in 1990,[1] Chris "really wasn't into the blues, I was into the guitar; I thought the music was old, dated," he admitted. "Prince was the only black guy that even held a guitar, the only person I could look out into the music business and see. I was a guitarist and needed someone to identify with, and as a black kid, Prince was really exciting to me. In America if you're young and black and play the guitar, they won't put you on the radio or TV. It's been like that since Elvis Presley."

It's not hard to understand why the teenage Chris felt frustrated. "Right across the street was a club where lots of my peer group would go and have dances, be with young girls and all that stuff," he told me. "And as for me? Well, I was playing on a Friday and Saturday night in a blues club with people that were old enough to be their grandparents!"

"But I was really fascinated with the music. It wasn't because my dad pressured me or wanted me to do it or anything. As a matter of fact, he didn't expect me to make music my main thing in life or anything; I think that he hoped I would get a 'real job' and be happy playing music on weekends.

"Of course, my friends all thought that it was pretty curious. They didn't know that I had a passion for blues and imagined that maybe I did it because my dad needed me to help out."

When Chris finally came up with his first album, to some ears *The Beginning* (1986) was a musical train wreck. Sub-Hendrix guitar riffs and down-home Lightnin' Slim Excello influences slammed together in a quirky gumbo, all anchored by the blues. The California-based Arhoolie Records specialized in releasing traditional roots-based music, so it was an unlikely home for *The Beginning*, but folklorist Nick Spitzer had brought Chris to the attention of owner Chris Strachwitz.

Recorded in Chris's small home studio with a drum machine used for most of the tracks, the album featured Chris on all the instruments, an approach he continued on most of his later albums. "They just said, 'Send me a tape. Record what you like and mail it to us.' They sent me back 600 bucks, which was a lot of money at the time, and I was just happy to have made a record." He laughed.

"The whole thing was a far better experience than when I found myself dealing with big corporations and they have you on the chopping block, trying to tell you what is the blues and what you should record."

With Robert Cray beginning to break, and the blues world hungry for the next young "blueblood," Chris found European promoters who'd been working with the older Baton Rouge performers and were eager to check him out. But at home, the blues mafia were not so kind. His was an altogether new take on the blues that they weren't used to hearing.

The album also brought him to the attention of Clifford Antone. Austin's Antone's club was the epicenter of blues in the U.S., with Stevie Ray Vaughan and the Fabulous Thunderbirds serving as keepers of the Texas blues flame. For Chris at the time, playing at Antone's seemed like a great opportunity.

Soon after relocating to Austin, he took off on a barnstorming stateside tour supporting Buddy Guy and Albert Collins. Clearly, Clifford Antone hoped that Chris would follow the classic blues route—it was obvious to everyone that, as a guitarist, he could more than hold his own with anyone out there. But it was not to be.

"When I lived in Austin, I was living in an apartment owned by Clifford, and I used to bump into Stevie [Ray Vaughan] all the time. He might come down to the club early in the afternoon when I was rehearsing with my band and hang out.

"He was a really nice guy, but he didn't dig my music because it was too funky for him. Really it was music from a different generation of musicians from his own influences, and it's a real shame that he didn't live to see where it might be going today. Back then he was doing a lot of shuffle stuff, but he never could understand that all I was doing was using those same Albert King licks into a kind of hip-hop attitude to playing."

Clifford Antone paid for Chris's recording time, and on a freezing February night in 1988, I sat with Chris in his car outside the club on Fifth Street as he played me a tape of the sessions. The mix of funk and soul originals owed more to Marvin Gaye than Jimmy Reed, and I wasn't surprised when he later told me that he and Antone's had parted ways.

"My problem has always been that promoters especially have always tried to pigeonhole my music. Because I'm black and have a blues background, I always end up playing with guys like Gatemouth Brown or they'll say, 'Hey, we got two dates for you in Chicago supporting Buckwheat Zydeco. . . .' Now, of course, I've got 100 percent respect for all those guys, but it's just not the right bill for me.

"I had to leave Antone's because they didn't consider what I was playing to be blues. When a white guy comes to me and says, 'Man, you're not playing the blues,' as though he's some kind of expert and knows what it's all about, then it's time for me to pack my bags and go anyway."

Having recently lost Robert Cray to a major record label, HighTone Records in California also became interested in working with Chris. The resulting album, *Cry of the Prophets,* largely made up from the Antone's tapes, was more ambitious than his first project. But while blues and soul remained Chris's bedrock, once again his music was too left field to satisfy HighTone's quest for a new Robert Cray.

"We got off to a good start. I went on tour around the country and they gave me tour support. My sound, as I saw it, was blues-guitar based but set around songs that were melodic rather than simply twelve bars. Everyone seemed pleased with what I was doing until I wrote a song I called '21st Century Blues.'

"My whole concept was that it should be a kind of rap blues, but when I came to demo the song for HighTone, they turned around and said I couldn't record it. Their problem was that they wanted to make me something I wasn't, but there's no way you can make anyone the 'next' anything. People like Robert Cray and Stevie Ray Vaughan weren't the 'next' anyone; the only way they achieved what they did was because they were both the first and they brought something original to the table and added something."

After being turned down by Sony, and by this time thoroughly disillusioned with the machinations of the American record industry, Chris left the U.S. He gigged in England with the rhythm section from Junkyard Angels, playing what he now called rap blues, with "21st Century Blues" the high point of every set. Surprising audiences who must have been expecting more traditionally blues based material, a dreadlocked Chris took them by storm.

"But I was absolutely broke, so after spending some time in London, I went to Copenhagen, where I met these two brothers, Thomas and Jakob Walbum, who played keyboards and drums. We started jamming and ended up recording most of the *21st Century Blues* album in a little Danish studio."

Around this time, Chris added King to his name. "I realized that I only had two first names, so I took the name King because of all the great things associated with it, especially in the blues."

English producer John Porter, who had recently finished working with Buddy Guy on his comeback album, *Damn Right, I've Got the Blues*, heard the tapes and arranged a record deal with a Los Angeles label, Private Music.

The release of *21st Century Blues . . . From Da Hood* kicked off a succession of fine albums that demonstrated to anyone without tin ears that there was very little that Chris couldn't handle. But while it did much to introduce his incandescent mix of rap and rock into mainstream rock, it only served to further distance Chris from the blues community.

"My blues was from another generation, so when I started rapping with my dreadlocks, a lot of people didn't understand that; they just saw me as someone really weird. But the truth is that everyone in my neighborhood dressed like that. I was the first guy in America to play a blues guitar and rapping, and the only difference now is that you have white kids doing it!

"The artists that I like are always the ones that have sincerity in their music, and that's what makes it genuine. When you hear Blind

Chris Thomas King with Clarence "Gatemouth" Brown (left) at the House of Blues, New Orleans, 1997 (Author's Collection)

Willie Johnson or Muddy Waters, you hear pure passion and a sense of truth in what they're singing, and that's what drew me into the blues in the first place.

"But I've got to sing and relate to what's going on in *my* world. That's my blues—there's no way that my blues should sound like the blues of the fifties, any more than Oasis should sound like Elvis Presley. Music is supposed to continue to grow and not be put in a bottle like some kind of time capsule."

When the Coen brothers picked Chris to appear in *O Brother, Where Art Thou?*,[2] ironically playing the part of a bluesman, his career made a quantum leap. As he was selected over some weighty competition— Keb' Mo', Taj Mahal, and Eric Bibb all apparently auditioned for the role—it's clear that Chris's long apprenticeship at the Blues Box had finally paid dividends.

"Acting is something that I always wanted to do, but I never imagined I would get the opportunity. At the time I realized I was going to be best known as an actor, I don't think a lot of people even knew I was a musician. They said, 'Yeah, looks like that guy can really play the guitar. . . .'

"When they began casting they tried some actors, but the Coen brothers wanted it to be really authentic. They wanted the character to be able to perform live on the camera and be a good actor, but they also wanted someone who was able to handle the guitar convincingly. And it was a comfortable role for me to play, because it was a character that I felt I knew, could relate to. The toughest thing was finding a voice, but I thought about Silas Hogan and Kelly; they held the key. Once I found that, the rest came naturally.

"My first day on the set they'd just cut my dreadlocks, and I prepared for the screen test rereading my lines. I came out of my trailer and this guy comes up to me real breezy in dusty overalls and is saying, 'Hi, boy, how're you doing?' etc. And it's George Clooney, the first guy I meet! Everyone knew that I was a rookie," he recalled with a laugh. "But they also knew that one weak link in the chain, and everything would be screwed up.

"We stayed in Jackson and then drove out to wherever we were shooting, which took about three months, and after a few weeks on the set the camaraderie between the Soggy Bottom Boys was really great. But they had a really tough time finding a crossroads that didn't have telegraph poles; it was the first time Hollywood had brought that whole myth to life, and they wanted it to be right.

"The most difficult thing that I had to do was to swim in the water and say my lines in the flood scene; the whole thing was filmed in a big tank at Universal Studios.

"I feel pretty good about the fact that I didn't screw it up and hope that when Eric Bibb sees me, he won't think I screwed it up. I didn't want to embarrass the blues community." Chris smiled.

"But I was lucky. If they'd written a role for a rapper, they would have found a whole lot of rappers out there, but there aren't a lot of younger black blues musicians that could have fitted the role."

Given the unprecedented success of *O Brother* and Chris's role portraying an acoustic bluesman, an obvious move might have been for him to throw himself into the acoustic fray. And indeed, hot on the heels of the movie, in 2001 Chris released an acoustic-oriented album, *The Legend of Tommy Johnson, Act 1: Genesis 1900's-1990's.* It was a curious mix, with Chris interpreting two stone-cold blues classics, Robert Johnson's "Canned Heat Blues" and Blind Willie Johnson's "Trouble Will Soon Be Over," before throwing in nine originals ranging from the stomping "John Law Burned Down the Liquor Sto'" to the electric Chuck Berry-style raunch of "Do Fries Go With That Shake?"

It all confirmed what many of us already recognized: Chris Thomas King was not a musician prepared to be typecast. He could play the heck out of the blues but was at home with just about anything you threw at him. This is fortunate, because Chris was soon part of the disparate troupe of acoustic musicians touring the show that became the Coen brothers' *Down from the Mountain* movie, a highlight being his performance of "John Law Burned Down the Liquor Sto'."

After playing a cameo role as Blind Willie Johnson in Wim Wenders' *The Soul of a Man,* part of Martin Scorsese's 2003 series celebrating the blues, Chris appeared the following year in the acclaimed biopic *Ray,* playing the part of Lowell Fulson.

"Maybe it's meant for me to be the bluesman at the cinema? Instead of the singing cowboy—maybe the singing bluesman?" he joked.

In 2005, Hurricane Katrina hit New Orleans. Chris lost his home and

Chris Thomas King with Tabby Thomas and the author at the New Orleans Jazz & Heritage Festival, 2009 (Author's Collection)

studio, and a few months later came the death of his mother, Jocelyn. These were devastating blows for him and his family, but with the resilience that has always marked his career, Chris used the disasters as inspiration. His 2006 album, *Rise,* featured a clutch of insightful original songs such as the soul-searching "What Would Jesus Do?" alongside unexpected versions of Joni Mitchell's "Big Yellow Taxi," "St. James Infirmary," and a particularly moving take of "What a Wonderful World." Chris Thomas King might have been down, but he sure as hell wasn't out.

Chris is still out there producing innovative albums and has played in just about every part of the known universe. He may be uncompromising, but as long as he's around, the blues is certainly never going to sound stale. Recently he was performing with a percussionist and tuba player.

"I've never shied away from being a blues artist. Unfortunately the public has, over the past hundred years, forgotten its true meaning and how revolutionary it was at the turn of the twentieth century. The blues planted the seeds for America's counterculture; it's quintessentially American music. I am proud to be its ambassador."

Kenny Neal at the Half Moon, London, 1988 (Courtesy of Paul Harris)

Chapter Eleven

Kenny Neal, Blues Right from the Bayou

When Kenny Neal jumped up onstage, and with a broad smile slammed into the introduction to Guitar Slim's "Things That I Used to Do," the roar of recognition from the audience at the 1988 Baton Rouge Blues Festival was the kind of enthusiasm you'd expect for a Prince song rather than a hoary old blues anthem written thirty-five years before.

Wrapped around his beaten-up blond Fender Telecaster, from the first bars Kenny clowned, playing the guitar behind his head or back and rubbing it against the microphone stand to mimic the sound of a slide guitar. Raful Neal's oldest son was performing as though his very life depended upon the success of his gig. Over the years I've caught Kenny Neal in action many times, and in 1990 he toured with my band in England. Always it was the same: no shucking, no time for lying back—just pure blues dynamite. But given his background, that's hardly surprising. Kenny comes from a family for whom playing music is as natural as breathing.

"I was born in 1957 in New Orleans Charity Hospital, born in the hallway! We lived in West Baton Rouge in a little town called Erwinville, but my family moved to the city in 1975. My grandfather was a preacher from Baton Rouge and moved to New Orleans after my grandmother died; my father was only two months old, and he and his sister were raised by an aunt. He didn't see his father until he was seventeen or eighteen years old.

"My dad got into playing harmonica after hearing Little Walter, thought, 'Hey—ain't going to work on the farm all my life; I'm going to play harmonica!' When he started out he'd fit all his band's gear—drums, amplifiers—into the trunk of his car; they didn't have a bass player. Buddy Guy played guitar with him but moved up to Chicago when I was about a year old.

"My dad would often come home about five or six o'clock in the

147

morning, and I used to sneak out to the car where all these musicians had left their instruments. I'd grab a guitar and jam on it until he'd wake up. Had a few ass whippings! 'Boy, you leave that guitar alone. You know that guitar isn't mine; it's Phil Guy's! You break it I gotta pay for it.' Back then, because Phil was young, my dad used to have to go and see his mother each time there was a gig and ask for permission for him to go!

"When I started school, the teachers loved me to death every time they had a talent show. I learned to read and write but didn't much care about what George Washington or Christopher Columbus had done, until report-card day came up. But I wasn't interested about what they were trying to put inside my head; I was thinking about the blues: Jimmy Reed and John Lee Hooker."

Kenny's dad would often bring him up onstage when he was playing, and from an early age there was no going back for Kenny. At school he learned to play the trumpet, but he didn't think the bass player in Raful's band was cutting it, so at the age of fifteen he muscled in on bass duties. The group included Rudolph Richard on guitar.

"Rudolph would call out all the notes to me every time we went to a change, and finally I figured it out and got pretty good. Rudolph began playing with my dad after Slim Harpo died—I would have been three or four years old at the time. My dad and Slim used the same trailer to haul the gear. Slim had a 1956 Buick he used to pull it, and when he wasn't working, my dad would borrow it.

"I got my first harmonica from Slim. One time he locked me up in the trailer for a joke, and I was banging on the doors crying, 'Let me out.' He came back and gave me one from his box—I will never forget that. But I moved on and began playing with Bobby Powell,[1] who was a blind soul singer. I wanted to get away from the blues, wanted to play what was going on in the Top 40 because it looked like that was what was happening."

When he was seventeen, Kenny received a message from Buddy Guy, who was short of a bassist and due to play Antone's in Austin, Texas. The club was the epicenter of the burgeoning Texas blues scene, with legendary shows by top blues artists such as Albert King and Muddy Waters. "I was playing at the Executive Club in Baton Rouge, when Phil [Guy] stuck a note in my pocket asking me to call Buddy. I called him during the break, and he told me to pack my suitcase, because he needed me to be in Austin three days later. I didn't even *have* a suitcase!" Kenny laughed.

"At the time, apart from Junior [Wells] and Philip Guy, Buddy had a drummer called Merle Perkins. I didn't really know what it was all about but caught a Greyhound bus as far as Houston and got to the gig. We didn't rehearse. Buddy just got up there and kicked off with 'Duh, duh, duh, duh duh duh duh,' and I said, 'Oh, man. So this is what they're talking about. Throw a rabbit in a briar patch.' I knew it all! Every song they played, my daddy had already showed me. I went back up to Chicago with Buddy, checked out the blues scene, and realized that there was a market for this music."

By the 1970s, the career of Buddy Guy and Junior Wells appeared to be on the ascendant. They'd toured as an opening act for the Rolling Stones, and Ahmet Ertegun had signed them to record an album for Atlantic Records. But as it happened, the greater success both men would enjoy in later life was still a pipe dream.

"We toured all across America, through Europe, and played Nice, Lyon, and Nancy," Kenny recalled. "But by this time I had changed my way of thinking. I realized there really was a market for blues music out there, the thing my dad had been telling me all along."

The most devastating blues music happens when there's a hint of danger—the musicians are on edge and songs career like runaway express trains. The late Junior Wells thrived on that particular mind set. He happily produced either dazzling performances or complete fiascos.

"Buddy and Junior Wells had their good nights, and like everybody they had their bad nights," Kenny admitted. "The only thing that ever messed me up was one time when we played Nice. There were 15,000 people out there and when Junior came out onstage, his head was kinda tight. He turned around and pointed a finger at me because he'd messed up real bad. I guess he figured that because I was only seventeen years old and we was in Europe, he could put it on the bass player.

"He goes, 'What are you doing? Follow me.' Everybody in the band knew I hadn't messed up, so I got really upset. He'd embarrassed me so bad in front of 15,000 people, the biggest crowd I'd ever played for. I said, 'Get me a ticket—you can damn well get me back to America!' But the next day we got on the bus to drive to the next town and he really apologized, so I felt better. Truth was he loved me like a son, and I stayed on for five years, so you know it wasn't that serious," Kenny said with a laugh. He stayed with Buddy Guy until 1980.

"The money wasn't good, but the people were," Kenny said. "Buddy and Junior are really nice. It messes me up when I go around the country and people say, 'Buddy Guy and Junior Wells—they just got drunk and didn't do a good job.' But they still pay to see them. Everybody has their problems and they're real people. I'm not a saint either!"

After leaving Buddy and Junior, Kenny lived in Canada for two years with his Italian first wife, but he admits it was tough musically. "Because I was unknown, no one would hire me. They only wanted to use Canadian bands. But I kept on doing what I was doing, and then one night I got lucky with a band called the Downchild Blues Band;[2] they were the hottest band in Canada, like the B. B. Kings of Canada. They needed a lead singer, saw me play in a club one night, and they said, 'Kenny, you've got a job.' They knew about my history of playing with Buddy Guy and Junior Wells and my dad and liked what I was doing. To be hired by them was instant promotion, and I stayed with the band for about two years. They paid me a good amount of money to front the show, and even now I'm still happy about what I did with them.

"We had a record deal set up, but that night that we were playing, the leader of the band, Donnie Walsh, just decided that he was gonna get messed up! He came up onstage and said, 'Hey, me and my old cousin Jack Daniel had a falling out tonight.' So, I'm there excited because we had a record company coming out to see us, and he goes out there and decides to fall off the stage. We had a whole row of people sitting out there, and I knew it was my big chance to show myself off because I was the lead singer."

After persuading his brothers Larry, Noel, Lil Ray, and Ronnie to join him in Canada, Kenny formed the first Neal Brothers Blues Band. "I eventually recorded an album with a guy called Pat Rush from Johnny Winter's band, which had me singing and playing guitar. We spent about thirteen thousand dollars on it, but it never got released."

But armed with the tracks he'd recorded, Kenny headed back down South to Baton Rouge, where he pressed up 500 copies of a single, one of which found its way to the desk of Bob Greenlee, the man behind Florida's King Snake Records. In 1987, he released Kenny's long-overdue first album, *Bio on the Bayou*, a potent blast of modern swamp blues.

The album was subsequently taken over by Chicago-based Alligator Records as *Big News from Baton Rouge!!*, and with Robert Cray flavor of the month, Kenny's arrival on the scene couldn't have been more timely.

"That first album of mine came about because Bob Greenlee came to the blues festival and checked me out," Kenny later told *Living Blues*.[3] "But I'll never forget where I come from, and I'll take all my homeboys with me. I don't care if somebody comes and puts 5 million bucks in my hand, because everything's going to be OK in my life anyway. I'd just like to see the musical part of it work and fulfill my life as a blues player. But if it don't happen real big, then I ain't worried about it. I play the blues; I don't live it. On the album I had Lucky Peterson from Bobby Bland's band playing keyboards, and Pete Carr was the engineer. Bill Samuel played horns, but I arranged them—he's my wife's brother. The album went over real well."

In 1991, Kenny appeared in a Broadway stage adaptation of Zora Neale Hurston and Langston Hughes' play *Mule Bone,* performing music by Taj Mahal. In the years that followed, he was unstoppable, headlining blues festivals all over the world and bringing out a string of fine albums. Along the way, he garnered countless awards, including a

Kenny Neal with Joe Louis Walker in London, 1988 (Courtesy of Paul Harris)

2005 W. C. Handy Award for an acoustic blues album, and in 2011 was inducted into the Louisiana Music Hall of Fame.

But the blues has never been an easy road to travel, and with family tragedies to cope with and a debilitating illness that saw him quit performing for a year in 2006, Kenny has certainly suffered more than his share of setbacks. Today he remains fiercely proud of both his family heritage and Louisiana blues and, as a performer, is that rare thing: a triple threat. A stunning guitarist and vocalist, following in his father's footsteps, Kenny is also a great harmonica player, producing a deep throaty sound unlike anyone else's on the block.

"I'm not really influenced by anybody in particular on guitar, but really I respect every other guitar player out there," he says. "I'd been brought up to play the way I'm feeling, and so the way I play is the way I feel. I'm not trying to copy anyone else. You might be able to ask some young kid that and he might even say, 'Kenny Neal,' but not me."

After a spell living in California, Kenny is now back in town, vowing that he'll put Baton Rouge's bluesmen back on the map. As long as he's around, the traditions that started out with Lightnin' Slim and Slim Harpo all those years before are certainly in capable hands. In 2015, the West Baton Rouge Museum organized an exhibition to commemorate the musical legacy of the Neal family.

Chapter Twelve

A Few Words on Lazy Lester

Lazy Lester's name has continually cropped up while I've been collating material, and so it should. J. D. Miller rightly loved him—without his input, many of the great Excello sides just wouldn't have been as funky. And he was the first Baton Rouge blues player to enter my life. So it would be a terrible omission not to put in a few words about him.

Maybe it was synchronicity, but in 1987, just as I was booking tickets for my Delta jet to Baton Rouge, record producer Mike Vernon phoned me. Mike's claim to fame is that he recorded the classic 1960s John Mayall albums featuring Eric Clapton and Peter Green, plus Fleetwood Mac, Chicken Shack, and just about every U.S. bluesman or woman who ever toured the U.K. Mike had a genius for recording blues and digging out neglected singers and even cut some sides in Baton Rouge. Albums issued by his defunct Blue Horizon label are now pricey collector's items.

Mike's reason for calling was that he was bringing Lazy Lester to the U.K., and given my experience of playing with blues guys on the road, he asked if I'd be interested in arranging for Lester to tour with my band, Junkyard Angels. As a bonus we'd also get to record with Lester, and the resultant album would be first in the renaissance of the Blue Horizon label. At this point I knew precious little about Lazy Lester, but after he arrived at my house clutching a tackle box that was home for his harmonicas, and a blue cooler for his beers, I soon found out.

And as it happened, we got along really well and most of the tour was a lot of fun. As anyone who knows Lester will agree, he's a loveable and entertaining character to be around.

The hard facts are these. Lester was born Leslie Johnson in 1933, in Torras, a small town near the Mississippi border. He moved to

Lazy Lester in England, 1987 (Author's Collection)

Scotlandville, where he held down a variety of jobs. As he told John Broven, he was working in a grocery store when he discovered his talent for playing the harmonica. "I was sitting on the bus going home one day, and I revved the harp up a bit. By the time I got off the bus at Scotlandville, I tuned the harp the way I wanted it and had learned to play Little Walter's 'Juke'—but Jimmy Reed was my favorite. I've got my own style and just kept foolin' around until I found the sound I wanted."

Lester formed a band, the Rhythm Rockers, but fate played a hand when he ran into Lightnin' Slim. "I met Lightnin' on a bus going to

Crowley, where he was due to make some recordings, and just went along with him. The guy that was supposed to play the harmonica, Wild Bill Phillips from Texas, didn't show up, so I told Lightnin' that from what I'd heard on his records, I believed I could do the same thing. So we got in the studio and it sounded all right."

Lester was soon making his own recordings, and his croaky vocals and sparse, lonesome harmonica graced fifteen Excello releases. Tracks such as "I'm a Lover Not a Fighter," "Sugar Coated Love," and "I Hear You Knockin'" were stone-cold swamp blues classics.

Along the way he was also the understated sonic architect of the Excello sound, not only adding his distinctive harmonica to many recordings but often playing washboard, "drumming" on a cardboard box with brushes, or the thumping on the saddle of Miller's horse.

Whatever it took, Lester did it. He also claims to have laid the concrete and whitewashed the walls of the studio's rudimentary echo chamber. But for the three weeks in May 1987 that we careered around England and Europe, I didn't know much of this. I did, however, get to know Lester and his songs pretty well. We had many adventures— including when, at a Dutch gig, he fell asleep during the break and resisted all attempts at revival.

Mike Vernon had painstakingly recorded a set of his songs that he hoped Lester would record. But the harp player showed little enthusiasm, and it was probably as big a surprise to Mike as anyone else that *Lester Rides Again* won a 1988 W. C. Handy Award.

Credit must also be given to the tenacity of Lester's manager, Fred Reif. A reticent, short, bearded man who looked more like a computer analyst than a manager for an idiosyncratic Louisiana harp player, Fred was the one who nailed down touring details with Mike Vernon. And when we met up in Baton Rouge, he was as excited about Lester's "comeback" as was the man himself.

Fred told me this all began three years before, when he sent Lester a bus ticket and suggested he come to his home in Pontiac, Michigan, to play a few local gigs. Reif, who managed Lightnin' Slim until his death in 1974, belongs to that elite, quirky band of blues fanatics without whose efforts the blues world wouldn't even begin to tick. But it would be a brave venture on everyone's part. Lester's track record was not exactly reliable.

Lazy Lester and the author at the Half Moon, London, 1987 (Author's Collection)

In the late sixties, an English promoter had arranged a tour for Lester, sent him an airline ticket, and been understandably dismayed when the singer failed to materialize at Heathrow Airport. When he made inquiries in Baton Rouge, all he could find out was that Lester had last been seen heading for the woods, with a fishing rod.

In view of Lester's apparent lack of interest in performing and some understandable indifference from potential promoters, it was fortuitous when the Fabulous Thunderbirds from Austin, Texas, recorded "Sugar Coated Love" and "I Hear You Knockin'," two of his finest Excello sides.

An appearance at the 1987 New Orleans Jazz and Heritage Festival alongside the Thunderbirds followed, and shortly afterwards Lester hit the trail to Antone's, Austin's home of the blues. After renewing his acquaintance with the band, Lester quickly became ensconced, telling anyone who would listen how much he'd like to record an album with Willie Nelson. He'd already met up with Willie's sister, who'd promised him a firm spot on the next album.

And to anyone who's heard Lester's early records, his desire to feature at the Grand Ole Opry should come as no surprise. Of all Jay Miller's records, with the exception of Slim Harpo's "Raining in My Heart," none sounded as country as Lester's. Just listen to the guitar licks.

A month after Lester appeared at the Chicago Blues Festival, Clifford Antone arranged for him to headline at an all-star jam at Antone's. Among others, the lineup would include the Thunderbirds, Stevie Ray Vaughan, Dr. John, and members of U2. But as the story goes, Lester had been partying for two days after his Chicago gig, failed to catch his flight, and later admitted that he "just didn't feel up to it."

Early one evening soon afterwards, I was sitting in the Blues Box when the telephone rang. Tabby answered and motioned me over.

It was Lester, back in town for the first time in nearly a year and looking for some action. He arrived an hour later, chauffeured by a pretty young girl who quickly exited.

Not much had changed since we last met: the same gangly figure, in a Coors baseball hat and a T-shirt proclaiming his identity in no uncertain manner. When we later got up to play at Estelle's Happy House out on Plank Road, it was clear that none of the kids realized that one of the city's greatest musical sons was in their midst.

Estelle's Happy House on Plank Road, Baton Rouge, 1987 (Author's Collection)

The next day, I met Lester at his brother's house. Huey and Alice live on North Fourteenth Street, a road lined with leafy sycamores, and Lester reminded me that we had talked about these trees when he was in England. For a man who imbibes beer as enthusiastically as he does, Lester remembers the finest details, and I feel guilty about my own shortcomings.

Huey and Lester reminisced about the local wildlife, Huey recalling as a child seeing snakes where he was playing. Lester topped this with a story about watching a king snake eat a rattlesnake. Cottonmouths are also pretty plentiful around these parts, he assured me. He pointed out a redheaded woodpecker and commented that the crows in Baton Rouge are much smaller than their English counterparts. I was surprised by Lester's powers of nature observation; he should be an ecologist.

We moved on to Kenny Neal's girlfriend's house. Crawfish were boiling!

"I started out listening to country-and-western music, and I hope I finish that way," Lester said.[1]

And the way he's going, it looks as though his wish will be fulfilled. We last met up in 2013. Lester was appearing about forty miles from where I live, in the small upstairs function room of a country pub deep in the heart of the Somerset Levels. It was an unlikely venue, and perched on a chair cradling an acoustic guitar, he cut a lonely figure.

I guessed that most of the well-heeled crowd had no idea who he was and, after hearing him strum through half a dozen Hank Williams songs, were probably none the wiser. At the time of this writing, he's still out there, and probably will be until he drops.

Notes

Introduction

1. In 1959, scholar Paul Oliver traversed the South, starting in Chicago, conducting field recordings that he later collated into his book and an accompanying album. When one looks back at his undertaking at that time, it's clear he was an extremely brave man.

2. Obtaining records of blues and R&B in England was very difficult. The major record companies ignored the genres until the arrival of the Rolling Stones, and then the idea dawned that there was money to be made. The selection remained limited, but strangely Woolworths offered a few cut-price albums and EPs by Lead Belly and Lightnin' Hopkins. Quite how or why has never been explained, but we pounced on them all.

3. Mississippi-born harmonica player Sonny Boy Williamson II toured England and Europe extensively in the early 1960s and became a much loved figure, recording with the Yardbirds, Brian Auger, and the Animals. A "colorful" character, Sonny Boy was so enamored with Britain that he took to wearing a specially tailored two-tone suit and a bowler hat and carried an umbrella and an attaché case for his harmonicas. While in England, he once set fire to a hotel room while attempting to cook a rabbit in a coffee percolator, and he allegedly stabbed a man in a street fight.

4. Lazy Lester, one of Excello Records' greatest acts, recorded "I'm a Lover Not a Fighter" and "I Hear You Knockin'," songs later recorded by British bands during the sixties "blues boom." In 1967, Lester toured with my band, Junkyard Angels, and we recorded *Lazy Lester Rides Again* for Blue Horizon Records. In 1988 the album received a W. C. Handy Blues Award. At the time of this writing, Lester is still going strong and regularly visits the U.K.

5. Clarence was a regular performer at the Blues Box. See note 1 in chapter 4 for more information.

Chapter One

1. Paul Oliver, *Conversation with the Blues* (1965; Cambridge: Cambridge University Press, 1997).

2. Slim Harpo wrote "I'm a King Bee," but as far as I or anyone else knew, the Rolling Stones could have written it themselves. The blues singers we knew were Muddy Waters, Howlin' Wolf, and Elmore James, and they all came from Chicago or Mississippi. Years later, Lightnin' Slim and Moses "Whispering" Smith would come to England, and by that time London R&B bands such as the Yardbirds and Pretty Things included Slim Harpo songs in their set lists.

3. Stella guitars, made by the Oscar Schmidt Company of Jersey City, New Jersey, and sold by mail order, became very popular during the early part of the twentieth century. With a high, trebly sound, they were ideal for playing blues music. Robert Johnson, Lead Belly, and Doc Watson all once played Stellas, as did Kurt Cobain on Nirvana's recording of "Polly."

4. Crossnote tuning, D-A-D-F-A-D, was a favorite of Skip James, who's credited with introducing the term.

5, Spanish tuning, D-G-D-G-B-D, is a common slide-guitar tuning and attributed to the eighteenth-century guitar instrumental "Spanish Fandango."

6. John Broven, *South to Louisiana: The Music of the Cajun Bayous* (Gretna, LA: Pelican, 1983).

Chapter Two

1. Sleeve notes and lyrics from Harry Oster's field recordings.

2. Robert Pete Williams, interview by Al Wilson, *Little Sandy Review.*

3. Robert Pete Williams, interview by Tam Fiofori, *Melody Maker.* It's interesting that a major music publication saw fit to include material about an obscure blues artist, sadly something unlikely to occur now.

4. Ibid.

5. A. J. Liebling, *The Earl of Louisiana* (Baton Rouge: Louisiana State University Press, 1970). Three-time Louisiana governor Earl Long was hugely popular, with a knack for connecting with the "common

people." His exploits were many and often racy. Earl demanded absolute loyalty from his inner circle, saying that he needed them to back him up not when he was right but when he was wrong. But he is probably best remembered for extending and completing the programs of social welfare begun by Huey Long. Whether or not you're interested in Louisiana politics, the book is a great read.

Chapter Three

1. Huey Long, "The Kingfish," was the controversial governor of Louisiana between 1928 and 1932 and a member of the U.S. Senate until his assassination in 1935. If you don't know anything about Huey, then check him out. He was a mercurial character who would have sucked Donald Trump into his vortex.

2. "Bad Luck Blues" brought Lightnin' Slim to the attention of the Chicago-based Chess Records, but although he apparently cut some sides for them, they were never released. Jay Miller signed Lightnin' Slim to an exclusive contract in 1955.

3. If you ever wondered what a "two-fisted mama" style of piano is, take a listen to Ms. Webster (January 11, 1936-September 5, 1999). The daughter of religious parents, she fell under the spell of Fats Domino and became a prolific session player at Jay Miller's studio. With a burgeoning solo career, she caught the ear of Otis Redding, who used her as his opening act for three years. In later life, she enjoyed a long recording career with Chicago's Alligator Records and was a regular performer at festivals throughout the world. rocking it out until the end.

4. Johnny Mars, from North Carolina, came to the U.K. in 1974 and made it his home. He still appears regularly.

5. Big Bear is a blues and jazz promoter and during the 1970s was instrumental in touring and recording many American blues artists in the U.K., including Lightnin' Slim, Whispering Smith, Cousin Joe, and Eddie Taylor.

6. Lightnin' Slim is buried in the Oak Hill Cemetery, Pontiac.

Chapter Four

1. Guitarist Clarence Edwards (March 25, 1933-May 20, 1993), one of fourteen children, originally appeared on recordings by Harry Oster for his Folk Lyric label, under the title of *Country Negro*

Jam Session with Butch Cage. An infrequent visitor to the Blues Box during my time, Edwards later hooked up with Steven Coleridge, who toured with him in the U.K. He recorded several albums—*Swampin', Louisiana Swamp Blues Vol. 4, Swamp the Word*, and *I Looked Down That Railroad*. His music was very much in the traditional Louisiana style, rarely venturing from the twelve-bar format.

2. Larry Garner, interview by Michalis Limnios, keepingthebluesalive. org, 2011.

3. Whispering Smith (January 25, 1932-April 28, 1984) worked with both Silas Hogan and Lightnin' Slim, with whom he toured Europe. His few recordings include "Texas Flood," immortalized by Stevie Ray Vaughan.

4. Tab Benoit (born in 1965, Baton Rouge) has carved a noteworthy niche for himself, pumping out a gumbo of down-home blues and swampy Cajun riffs infused with a heady dash of Chicago blues. A spontaneous and fiery player, he's a credit to the Blues Box finishing school.

5. John Lisi is now New Orleans based and heads up Delta Funk. In 2009 he received the Slim Harpo Award for Blues Pioneer.

Chapter Five

1. Mick Jagger quote from *Rolling Stone* magazine.

2. Slim Harpo, interview by Jim Delehant, *Hit Parader*, 1969.

3. Slim Harpo, interview by Max Jones, *Melody Maker*.

4. Lightnin' Slim, interview by Max Jones, *Melody Maker*.

5. The legendary Scene club, on West Forty-Sixth Street in Manhattan, was owned by Steve Paul and notably featured nights with Jimi Hendrix and the Doors. Paul went on to become Johnny Winter's manager.

Chapter Six

1. Guitar Slim (December 10, 1926-February 7, 1959), born plain Eddie Jones in Greenwood, Mississippi, is best remembered for his song produced by a young Ray Charles, "The Things That I Used to Do." He was hugely influential on everyone from Buddy Guy to Johnny Guitar Watson to Stevie Ray Vaughan, and just about any Southern blues guitarist worth his salt knows the introduction to "The Things That I Used to Do," even if he doesn't include the song in his repertoire.

2. Lonnie Brooks (1933-) cut his teeth playing with Clifton Chenier in the mid-fifties, before recording for the Goldband label based in Lake Charles. His notable singles included "The Crawl," recorded by the Fabulous Thunderbirds, and "Family Rules." He was once dubbed "the human jukebox" because of his ability to play in many styles. He relocated to Chicago in 1960, where he developed his career under the name Lonnie Brooks, recording for the Alligator label. Among his claims to fame is being featured in two Heineken commercials.

3. Influenced by Texas players Gatemouth Brown and T-Bone Walker, Long John Hunter spent his years ducking beer bottles in border bars before eventually being "discovered" by Alligator Records in 1996.

4. Lonnie Brooks, interview by D. Thomas Moon, *Living Blues,* March 1998.

5. Philip Walker (February 11, 1937-July 22, 2010) was born in Louisiana and raised in Texas. He joined the band of the zydeco king Clifton Chenier in 1955 and played and toured with him extensively for the next three and a half years. He later moved to California, where he was highly respected, recording for Bruce Bromberg's HighTone label.

6. Accordion player Clifton Chenier (June 25, 1925-December 12, 1987) fused the music of his black Cajun culture with rock and even pop. As he once put it, "I was the first one to put the pep to it." And that he certainly did, often playing four-hour sets without break!

Chapter Seven

1. Art Rupe (1917-) founded Specialty Records, the most successful and influential of the West Coast labels. Sam Cooke, Little Richard, Joe Liggins, Guitar Slim, and Larry Williams were among his artists.

2. Johnny Vincent (October 3, 1927-February 4, 2000) was a record producer for Art Rupe at Specialty Records but in 1955 founded Ace Records in Jackson, Mississippi. In 1956, he branched out from recording local blues artists and began recording New Orleans R&B bands, notably Huey "Piano" Smith and the Clowns.

3. Between 1955 and 1960, Fats Domino (February 26, 1928-) produced twenty-two singles that sold more than a million copies each, a total only surpassed by Elvis Presley.

4. Lyrics from "Hot Seat Blues" and "Welfare Blues" are reproduced with the kind permission of Flat Town Music. Writer: Ernest J. Thomas, Publishers: Flat Town Music (BMI)/Blue Eagle Music (BMI).

Chapter Eight

1. *Blues Breakers with Eric Clapton,* recorded in 1966, is arguably one of the most influential records in rock history. The list of guitarists inspired by Clapton's particularly dense, overdriven sound is endless and includes Peter Green, Jimmy Page, Billy Gibbons, Eddie Van Halen, and just about anyone who ever picked up a Gibson Les Paul guitar.

2. "The Thrill Is Gone," written in 1951 by Roy Hawkins and Rick Darnell, reached No. 6 on the *Billboard* charts, but B. B. King's 1969 recording was the number for which he became best known, reaching No. 16 on the *Billboard* pop charts and providing him with that elusive "crossover" success.

3. The Flyright record label, established in the U.K., specialized in repackaging vintage Excello recordings gleaned from the vaults.

Chapter Nine

1. Jackie Neal would later achieve considerable success with her album *Down In Da Club,* only to die in 2006, murdered by an ex-boyfriend.

2. Invented in 1949, the tough Shure "Green Bullet" microphones were originally designed to be used in takeout-type food shops or at sports events and were often found suspended from the ceilings of burger joints for easy access. Over the years their unique qualities—rugged, with a sensitive midrange and an on/off switch—made them a favorite of harmonica players the world over.

3. Freddy Below (September 6, 1926-August 13, 1988) was a house drummer at Chess Records in Chicago and incredibly influential, credited with coming up with the style of blues drumming we know today.

4. Junior Parker (March 27, 1932-November 18, 1971), born near Clarksdale, was an original member of the ad hoc group the Beale Streeters, with B. B. King and Bobby Bland. His records "Feelin' Good" and "Mystery Train"—the latter covered by Elvis Presley—are credited with helping lay the foundation for what we now know as rockabilly.

Chapter Ten

1. Tabby Thomas, interview by Peter Lee and David Nelson, *Living Blues,* May 1990.

2. Set in 1937 in rural Mississippi, the movie is a satire loosely based on Homer's epic poem "The Odyssey" and grossed over $71 million. Chris played the part of Tommy Johnson, based on the character of Robert Johnson.

Chapter Eleven

1. Bobby Powell (born 1941) started out as a blues singer, with several releases on Shreveport's Whit Records in the 1960s. His 1966 recording of "C. C. Rider" topped the *Cash Box* R&B charts. He changed direction in the 1970s, registering several regional hits with his soul records. When I met him in 1988, Bobby had given up performing and worked for three churches in Baton Rouge as musical director.

2. Formed in Toronto in 1969 by brothers Donnie and Richard Walsh, the band, now known simply as Downchild, still performs. Over the years they have used 120 musicians!

3. Kenny Neal, interview by Jim Traseger, *Living Blues,* May 1990.

Chapter Twelve

1. Broven.

Index